# THE NIGHT GIFT

OTHER BOOKS BY PATRICIA A. MC KILLIP

*The House on Parchment Street*

*The Throme of the Erril of Sherill*

*The Forgotten Beasts of Eld*

# THE NIGHT GIFT

Patricia A. McKillip

Illustrated by Kathy McKillip

AN ALADDIN BOOK
*Atheneum*

*For my cousins,*
*whose voices I borrowed.*
*Thanks again.*

*Published by Atheneum*

*Published simultaneously in Canada by*
*McClelland & Stewart, Ltd.*
*Manufactured by Fairfield Graphics, Fairfield, Pennsylvania*
*ISBN 0-689-70470-4*
*First Aladdin Edition*

# THE NIGHT GIFT

We went to the library from Barbara's house: Claudia Gill and Barbara Takaota and I. Briar Avenue was an old street; you could tell by the sidewalk, which didn't lay flat anymore but bumped up and down in the air. In front of the deserted house, two slabs of cement, pushed up by a tree root, made an upside-down V, so first you walked up one side and then down the other, which is not what you expect to do on a sidewalk, especially in high Swedish clogs. But I always liked the sidewalk and the rambly, untrimmed hedges and the little old houses on Briar Avenue that were so different from houses in an ordinary neighborhood. Barbara was quiet; I didn't know then what she wanted to tell us. Claudia was talking about an operation she was going to have for her face. I was listening to her out of the corner of my mind, and watching some Mexican kids riding tricycles on the bumpy sidewalk. They were all little and round, and I was trying to remember the first time I had ridden on a tricycle.

"Let's go to the park after the library," Barbara said suddenly, breaking into Claudia's voice, but Claudia didn't mind since she was only half-listening to herself anyway.

"Okay." I was supposed to go straight home from the library to do a report on *The Scarlet Letter,* which was due the next day. But the late sun was sitting on the hills winking between the walnut branches, and the air was so still not even the walnut leaves were moving, so I couldn't worry about *The Scarlet Letter*. Claudia took the words out of my mind, which startled me.

"*The . . . Scarlet . . . Letter,*" she said softly. She was born with a cleft palate, and every once in awhile she got very depressed about her face, which the doctors still hadn't finished. Her upper lip was flat and pulled up towards her nose, and you could see more of the underside of her nose than you would ordinarily expect. Her voice sounded hollow, and honked a little sometimes like a goose's voice, so in her classes at school she never said anything. She did her talking with us. "Scarlet. I love that word. In *Gone with the Wind* the heroine's name was Scarlett O'Hara. I wish they had named me Scarlett instead of Claudia. Claudia sounds like a mud pie."

"It does not," I said.

"It sounds like clod and dough, which is a mud pie."

That made me giggle. It was a good evening to laugh in, with blackbirds and sea gulls wandering around in the sky, and people you couldn't see making little splashes of sound in the air, and Neil Brown just locking his ten-speed at the library door. I glanced at Barbara to see if she had seen him, but she was frowning at the sidewalk.

"I like Claudia."

"I don't like it," Claudia said, "because it belongs to me."

So I glanced at her to see if she were going to be depressed, but she was just stating a fact. Neil had gone inside the library. Barbara was still walking slowly, with her fingers under her arms. Usually she walked as though she were trying to get a little ahead of herself, with her long black hair flying out behind her. I knew something was on her mind, but I couldn't guess what. Usually I knew exactly what she was thinking.

We reached the library, a bright, rather noisy, one-floor building about as old as the town. The tables were crowded with kids doing homework. At one of the tables on the adult side of the library I saw Neil. He had just sat down and was opening his notebook. Barbara had gone to the children's section because she had promised to get the twins some picture books. So I went over to talk to Neil, with Claudia following behind me like a shadow.

"Hello," I said cheerfully. He blinked up at me, his eyes

full of whatever he was reading. Then he smiled.

"Hi, Joslyn." He saw Claudia behind me and nodded. "Claudia."

"Hi," Claudia whispered, and without looking at her, I knew her face was bright red. Neil was two grades ahead of us, vice-president of the junior class; he made the honor roll every semester and played on the basketball team even though he was a little short. But he had seen her enough at my house to know her name. He put his pen down politely, and I said, "What are you doing?"

"Political science. Cramming for a test tomorrow. You come to study?"

I moved to look over his shoulder at his notes. They were incomprehensible. "No, I have to check out *The Scarlet Letter* because I left my copy at school. I have to make an oral report on it tomorrow about Hester, whoever she is."

"You haven't read it yet?"

"It slipped my mind."

His brows crooked, peaking over his eyes. "Joslyn, you shouldn't let things slide like that. That's a rough book."

"Well, I have all night."

"You and Brian." He smiled again, even though he was still frowning a little. "Is your brother going to be home tonight?"

I nodded. Neil had shaggy, ivory-colored hair, and light, vivid eyes that made me think, while I was looking at him, of snow and skiing and fiords, so I didn't really hear his question. I said after a moment, "What?"

"What's Brian doing tonight?"

"Oh. I don't know. I never know what he's going to do. Drop by and see."

"I will, thanks." His eyes strayed to his notebook, and I straightened.

"Well, I'd better go. Good luck on your test."

"Thanks. I'll see you, Joslyn. Bye, Claudia." I heard a page in his notebook rattle as I turned. He was the nicest person I knew except for Barbara. I had liked him ever since he'd come home with my brother the first day of their freshman year; he'd been like a second, much more cheerful, older brother. Then one day I'd looked at him and realized, with a funny feeling in my stomach as though a fish had jumped in it, that the last thing I wanted was another brother.

We joined Barbara and she said, "Did you find it?"

"What?"

"*The Scarlet Letter.*"

"Oh. No. Just a moment."

She went to check out her books, and I went to look under Hawthorne. *The Scarlet Letter* wasn't there, which shook me a little until I realized that if it wasn't there, I didn't have to do my report.

Claudia said nervously, "Joslyn, you have to do it—you're flunking English."

"Well, how can I do the report if I can't find the book?" I asked reasonably.

"Well, you have to do it."

"Well, I can't." We went to the main desk, where Barbara, looking at my empty hands, came out of her thoughts.

"Did you check the paperbacks and the sorting shelf?"

So I checked and found it on the paperback rack. It was not a very thick book, and that cheered me. I checked it out, and we left. Passing the window, I saw Neil inside, twirling his pencil in his hair, his lips moving. From a distance he looked thin, but up close I could see the tension of hard muscle in his arms and neck. I felt hollow for a moment, looking at him. Then we passed the window.

We stopped at Barbara's house to drop off the books, then went down two blocks to the park. It was a small park bounded on three sides by houses and on the fourth by a thick hedge and chain link fence that hid the freeway. Standing in the middle of it, I always felt as if I were in the center of the world, because the sky fit the trees circling it like a lid.

We lay down on one of the little hills that looked like burial mounds at the side nearest the freeway. We were surrounded by sound. The traffic honked and sped and screeched on the freeway. A baseball game was in progress at one corner of the park; we could hear the hollow conk of the bats, and people whistling and shouting. College students thwacked tennis balls on the courts near us; kids were playing on the swings and slides; now and then their high voices flashed to us. But if I looked up at the huge circle of sky, it seemed to drown the noise. The sun was still hovering over the hills, and the shadows of young pine stretched taut as rubber bands across the grass. My clogs slid off, and I put *The Scarlet Letter* under my head. Even Claudia, on one side of me, was quiet. Then Barbara, lying on her stomach with her face on her arms, said softly to no one, "My brother is coming home."

I turned my head to look at her. She rested her chin on her hands and stared at the car-flicks in the hedge. Her face was quiet, faraway; usually it was never still for long.

"When?" Claudia asked.

"Next month."

"Is he better?"

"I guess so, or they wouldn't let him come home. I'm not sure if he's staying."

Joe Takaota was my brother's age. Last fall, just after school started, he had been standing in front of a window in his room, just looking out at the rain. Mrs. Takaota had asked him if he had any dirty laundry. For a moment he hadn't said anything. Then he said, "It's so ugly," and pushed his hands through the glass. Since then he had been in a hospital, and Barbara had only seen him once. She rolled over then, onto her back, her arms outstretched, and looked at the sky. Her face looked more familiar.

"I wish . . ." she said softly. "I wish . . ."

"What?"

"I wish I knew why he did it." She never talked about him very much. "I wish I could make a place for him, just for him, where he could go when he was depressed, that was so beautiful, that just being in it would make him happy. Just standing in it would make him forget ugly things, like when you stand in a forest, or by the sea, only even more beautiful than that. . . ." Her hands, above her head, had closed into fists.

"Where would you make it?" I asked. "How?"

Her hands opened. She looked at me, her face opening in a smile. "I don't know. What time is it?"

"Almost six."

She rolled to her feet. "I have to go help with dinner."

We walked back slowly. I thought of Joe Takaota, small-boned and dark like Barbara, with his straight hair falling over his face. The year they started high school, he and my brother had been together a lot. But after that they had grown apart.

Claudia, bumping against me as she walked, said, "This is my favorite time—twilight."

"It's not twilight until after the sun sets," I argued, but she ignored that.

"Twilight," she whispered. "Twilight. It sounds like an echo."

We followed Barbara into her kitchen. Her mother was making spaghetti, and the twins were sitting on the kitchen floor with all the books Barbara had gotten for them. They were in first grade, and they looked like a pair of Geisha dolls. Mrs. Takaota gave us a smile through the steam from the spaghetti. She taught fifth grade in the school where the twins went. The twins, Sara and Kim, got up and came over to us. Claudia ducked behind me a little. She was shy of them because they would stare at her face and they were apt to say anything. But they had only come over to investigate my clogs. Sara stood on my feet and grabbed for my hands.

"You're too tall," she commented. She stuck her face against my stomach and measured herself against me with one hand. "I come up to here on you."

"Sara, get off Joslyn's feet," Mrs. Takaota said. "Go help Barbara set the table."

I walked a few steps with Sara on my feet. Kim hung beside me, wanting a turn, so I gave her one while Mrs. Takaota talked to Claudia, and Barbara sat at the table reading one of the twins' library books. Mr. Takaota was dead, so Mrs. Takaota had to work, which left Barbara having to take care of the twins and help with housework a lot. She finished the book and got down to business.

"Sara, Kim, get the books off the floor and take them to your room. Then go get washed. Mom, I need a dollar to buy some music."

"Get one out of my purse," Mrs. Takaota said absently, listening to Claudia. She was one of the rare people Claudia talked to besides us.

"They're going to straighten my nose," Claudia said. "And do something to the roof of my mouth. I hope it's the last one."

"That's wonderful," Mrs. Takaota said, dumping spaghetti sauce on the spaghetti. "Do you girls want some dinner?"

I thought of *The Scarlet Letter* and sighed. "I'd better not. Thanks anyway. I have to do homework."

Barbara, rattling silverware onto the table, looked at

me and grinned. "You'd better have it done, Joslyn. You know what Mr. Frank will say."

"I know. I know. It's not just reading a book that's important, it's the principles behind it. Discipline. Mental Exercise. Appreciation of Art. Things I may not comprehend now, but later I will be grateful for having—having—"

"Nurtured," Claudia said.

"Ah, yes. Nurtured. Blah."

"Even so," Barbara said, "you don't want to flunk out of freshman English, so you'd better read it."

"I will," I promised. "Come on, Claudia. Good-bye, Mrs. Takaota. Bye, Barbara."

"See you tomorrow."

I dropped Claudia off at her house on the next block, then walked across the park and up the freeway overpass. I stopped at the top a moment to watch the cars. The sun had gone down and the hills to the east were blurring into the sky. Beneath me the freeway ran like a river with a swift current of work traffic. On Barbara and Claudia's side of the freeway, the city was Campbell, but where I lived it turned into San Jose. Campbell melted into San Jose, and San Jose spilled over into Santa Clara and Cupertino and Los Altos, which merged into Palo Alto and Stanford, and so on, north up the freeway, cities running into cities until they all ran into San Francisco, which was stopped by the ocean. If you looked down from the hills on a clear night, you could see the lights sprawled like a galaxy of stars in the darkness from the mountains at one end to the bay at the other. In the darkness it was beautiful. But during the day, sometimes all you could see was a motionless, yellow mess of air.

I thought of Joe Takaota on the way home until I saw Neil Brown's bicycle locked to our mailbox. I went in. He and my brother were sitting in the living room listening to a record. Brian had his guitar; he was trying to play along with the music. He had no shirt on and he was smoking, two things that annoyed our mother. He had dropped out of school on his birthday, but he and Neil were still good friends.

"Hello again," I said. Neil gave me a nod and a smile, but Brian, cross-legged on the floor, shook the light hair out of his eyes and glowered at me.

"You," he said, "are an unmitigated pest."

I made a mental note to ask Claudia what unmitigated meant. "Now what?" I said, sighing resignedly.

"What? What, indeed. You broke my 'Fair, Far Days' album."

"I did not."

"You did, too."

"I did not."

"People's Exhibit Number One." He picked up a record jacket and shook it. About fifteen pieces of record fell out. I stared at it, fascinated. Brian blew a cloud of smoke up at me. "Prosecution rests. You owe me seven dollars."

"I do not! I did not!"

"I found it in your room. All sixty pieces of it."

"All I did was play it. I didn't drop it, or step on it, or—" Then I stopped. I had listened to a song that morning, then I had put it back in the jacket and sat down on Erica's bed to put my socks on. I must have left it on the bed, half-hidden in the sheets, for Erica to bounce down on. Thinking of that made me giggle, even though I was upset. Brian held out his hand.

"Seven bucks."

"I didn't break your record and I haven't got seven dollars!" He made me so mad I wanted to kick him, for embarrassing me in front of Neil. I turned; I heard him swear at me as I went into the kitchen. No one was there. A note on the refrigerator said "Out to dinner. Stew on stove." So I ate stew I couldn't taste, while I could hear their voices murmuring, laughing in the living room.

I could smell lilac from the open window in my bedroom when I went in. I pulled the covers up over my bed and lay down and tried to concentrate on *The Scarlet Letter*. I read ten pages of it, then I closed my eyes. I could not comprehend how anyone could write such a boring book. I dragged my eyes open and read another page.

When I opened my eyes again, the room was black. I heard Erica breathing in the bed next to me. I had a groove on my cheek from sleeping on the backbone of the book. I switched on my lamp, and Erica rolled over and put the sheet over her head. I got up and went to the kitchen for a glass of water. The whole house was dark.

While I was drinking, the phone rang, and I almost choked. It was beside the cupboard, so I grabbed it before the second ring and said, "Hello?"

"Joslyn?"

My voice woke up. "Barbara? What's the matter?" The clock over the stove said five after one, but she didn't seem concerned with time.

"Joslyn. You remember what I was talking about in the park?"

Somehow, I wasn't surprised at what she was going to say. "Yes."

"Well, I'm going to do it. I don't know where yet, or how, but I'm going to do it."

"Okay. I'll help. So will Claudia."

"Okay. But it will be a secret place, just for him, so don't tell anyone."

"I won't."

"Thanks, Joslyn. I know we can do it. I know we can."

"Of course we can."

"Okay. Thanks. Good-bye."

She hung up. I went back upstairs and undressed, and tried to read, but all I could think of, like a song that kept running in and out of my head, was that somewhere, somehow, we were going to make a place that was the most beautiful place in the world.

The next day a scientific miracle occurred. There was a fire drill during English, so that by the time we all filed out and stood in the yard awhile, then filed back in and got lectured by Mr. Frank for talking during the drill, the period was over and my oral report was postponed until Monday. That cheered me up for the whole day. I told Claudia at lunch what we were going to do, and of course she thought it was a good idea. And then I saw Neil for a moment after school when I was putting books in my locker, and he spoke to me as though he didn't remember the stupid argument he had sat through. So, going home in the warm Friday afternoon, with the sun dripping off trees and turning Claudia's nose pink, I felt as if my blood were full of champagne bubbles, and I was ready to do anything.

"We have to find a place," Barbara said. Then her eyes came down out of the trees and she turned to me. "Joslyn, you have to read that book! You said you were going to have it done for today."

"I fell asleep. It wasn't my fault. Nobody has a right to force somebody to read a boring book."

"I liked it," Claudia said.

"You would."

"I don't care if it is boring," Barbara said. "If you don't pass English, you'll have to go to summer school four hours a day for six weeks."

The thought chilled me. "I'll read it," I promised.

"It's a love story," Claudia said. "You'll like it. The heroine was ostracized—"

"She was what?" I said, startled.

"Ostracized. You know, nobody would speak to her because she had a child out of wedlock. Wedlock. That's a funny thing to call marriage. Wed. Lock."

"Claudia, we have to think of a place," I said, so she let wedlock alone and applied her mind to more immediate things.

"A place in the mountains."

"It has to be a place he can get to quickly," Barbara said. "Besides, how would we get there to make it?"

"Well, where is there a beautiful place around here?"

"It doesn't have to be beautiful to start out with—we'll make it beautiful. We'll put the most beautiful things we can find in it, so the moment he walks into it he'll forget—"

"Forget what?" Claudia said. Barbara's hair swished suddenly as she shook her head. Her face was puckered.

"If I knew," she said softly. "If I could understand."

I said comfortingly, "We'll do it. We can do it." I trailed my hand across a juniper bush and broke a twig off to sniff it. It smelled like the mountains on a wet day. Across the street, a little old lady with a straw hat on her head was watering her garden. Her screen door had a hole in it, as if it had been kicked, and the paint was peeling off her house, but the garden was beautiful with fuschia, roses, daisies, sunflowers, rows of marigolds, coral bells, and the tiny white flowers I never could remember the names of. I had said hello to her once across her fence, but she had just looked at me, her mouth all folded together as if she had forgotten to put her teeth in. It made me laugh thinking about that, and Barbara's face lifted out of her hair, smiling again.

"What?"

"Nothing. There's a place, but I bet she won't let us borrow it."

Barbara looked across the street. She stopped, almost in surprise, so that we all bumped to a halt on the sidewalk. She gripped my arm.

"Joslyn?"

She made my name a question. Then I saw what she was

looking at, and I knew what she was asking. I said incredulously, "That?"

Claudia was doing a little dance behind us. "What? What are you looking at?"

"That house," Barbara said. Her fingers were still tight on my arm; she was staring at the deserted house as if flowers and paint were blooming across its walls under her eyes.

Claudia said in a small voice, "But it's so ugly."

"What," I said practically, "if someone owns it? Besides which, it is right down the street from the police station."

"I want to go in it," Barbara said. I glanced up and down the street.

"There are twenty thousand people out."

"They won't see us. Those big pine trees practically block the whole front yard. I just want to look in a window." She turned to us, pleading. "It doesn't matter what the outside looks like, does it? It's just a tiny old house no one wants—look at the broken window, and the way the porch steps are falling apart. No one cares about it. They won't mind if we borrow it. We could just borrow one room in it—just one room." She stopped, her eyes flicking over our faces. When we didn't say anything, she said, "I can't think of any other place. I can't."

"It's trespassing," Claudia said. "Breaking and entering."

"Not," I said, "if we can pick the lock."

Barbara let go of my arm finally. "Is it all right? The only other place I can think of is his bedroom, and that's where he hurt himself. Besides, the twins would come and play in it."

I looked at the house. It was set back in a circle of dark, shaggy pine, so almost all you could see was the door and the porch, which were paintless and sad. There were no flowers, not even a lawn; only dirt and tufts of long stray grass. The only nice thing about it was the soft purple masses of lilac flowing down from a trellis over the porch. I caught a whiff of it as we stood there. I never could resist lilac.

"All right," I said. "But I think we should wait till it's dark."

"So do I," Claudia said. I could tell from her face that she didn't care for Barbara's idea, but she seemed resigned. "I just hope we don't all get thrown in jail. I have an operation in six weeks."

"If anyone sees us, we'll just explain," Barbara said. "Anyway, no one will."

"Besides," Claudia added belatedly, turning to me, "it is too breaking if you pick the lock."

"I don't see why, if we don't break anything. But it doesn't matter anyway, because none of us can pick locks."

"We won't break anything," Barbara said softly. "We won't hurt anything, disturb anything. We'll just borrow a room and make it beautiful. Does that sound illegal?"

Claudia smiled suddenly, which made me realize how little she did that. "No."

We separated then until evening: Barbara had to go to her flute lesson, and Claudia was going shopping with her mother. I had nothing more exciting than *The Scarlet Letter* to occupy myself with, so I walked home slowly, stopping for a brief swing in the park after making sure no one I knew was watching. At home, I found my mother, whom I hadn't seen in two days, in the living room, dressed in a long skirt and a flowered blouse. She was vacuuming, and she switched off the sound when I came in.

"Hello," I said cheerfully. "You look nice."

"Hello," she said. "Why didn't you tell me you were flunking English?"

I sighed. "Mother," I said reasonably, "everyone flunks something in their freshman year, getting used to new studying habits, et cetera—"

I heard a long, drawn-out, "Bullshit," behind me. Brian, lounging in, lit a cigarette and gestured with it. "Don't rationalize. First you flunk English, then English and science, then English, science, history and volleyball; and first thing you know, you've rationalized yourself out of school. I know."

"If you're so smart," I said, "why aren't you back in school?"

"I'm not that smart."

"Don't smoke in my living room," our mother said irritably. Our father came in then, wearing a coffee-colored suit and a cigarette in his mouth.

"Are you ready?" he said to her. She sighed. He swept a lean finger at me.

"You get some studying done this weekend. I don't want you to go anywhere; I want you to stay in this house and study."

"But, Dad—"

"No. I mean it. You study."

"But, Dad," I wailed. Then I had a burst of genius. "Can't I at least go to the library and get some books I need for class?"

He eyed me, but found nothing suspicious in my demeanor. "All right. You go there; you get what you need, and come right back. No detours."

"Yes, sir. Where are you going?"

"We're going to a dinner in San Francisco," my mother said. "There's a casserole in the oven; it'll be done in a few minutes. Don't forget it."

"Abandoning your children again," Brian commented. "Can I borrow your car tonight?" He had only a learner's permit. Mom smiled at him.

"Very funny, Sweetie. Either put that cigarette out or go outside. You know the rules."

"Nag, nag, nag," Brian said mildly, putting it out.

"Where are you going?" Dad said.

"To a party at Neil's."

Instantly all reason vanished from my head. "Oh, can I go?" I begged, clutching the vacuum. "Please? He has neat parties—everyone says so, and I want—" I stopped dancing with the vacuum abruptly at their expressions. My brother said frostily, "You weren't invited."

My father said frostily, "You are to stay home and study. You should learn to listen."

My mother said frostily, "You heard your father. Besides, I don't want Erica alone all evening. And since you're standing there with the vacuum in your hand, you can finish the rug."

I had never, as I switched on the vacuum, felt so much like Cinderella in my life. But I cheered up gradually as I worked. After all, the deserted house wasn't exactly a detour, and Erica would be perfectly all right left to herself for a few minutes. Neil would have other parties, and one of these days he would wake up to the fact that I was no longer just Brian's kid sister. I was standing in a corner, vacuuming one spot over and over again, and thinking of how Neil's eyes turned to you and stayed on your face while you spoke, his white brows peaking a little over his eyes in concentration, when Erica slammed the door behind me and said, "Phew. What's that smell?"

I jumped. Then I bounded for the kitchen. The casserole was burnt black; it smoked as I drew it out of the oven.

Erica said, looking at it, "What was it?"

It looked vaguely green. "I don't know. The inside is probably good."

She turned away. "Forget it. I'll make a sandwich. Do you know what that stupid Martin Shane did to me today?"

I put the casserole in the sink and turned the water on. The whole thing hissed a cloud of steam like a dragon at me. "I have no interest," I said coldly, "in what Martin

Shane did to you. Did you know you broke Brian's 'Fair, Far Days' album?"

"You left it on my bed," she said composedly. "Anyway, Liz Cramer sat on it, not me. Martin Shane dove right on top of me at swim practice. I've got a bump on the back of my head, and his eyebrow was cut. Feel." She turned her head. "You can feel it."

I felt around in her hair. Normally it was as pale as mine, but since she started swimming on the team at her school in earnest so that she could break Mark Spitz's record at the Olympics, it had turned a sort of pearly green. I found the lump at the base of her neck.

"You really should wash your hair sometimes."

She twitched away from me. "I do. Where are Mom and Dad?"

"San Francisco."

"I'm staying overnight at Liz's tonight. Her mom's going to drive us to the swim meet tomorrow morning."

"How nice."

"Can I borrow your—"

"No."

"Joslyn! I left my tennis shoes at school, and I have to borrow yours. Please?"

"They're too big."

"No, they aren't." She wiffled her bare toes at me. "I have big feet."

She did. I sighed. "All right. But they're brand new, and if you lose them, I'll skin you alive."

"I won't lose them," she said contemptuously.

"Ha," I said with feeling. "Remember my blue sweater and my friendship ring that I never saw again after you borrowed them?"

She banged an empty water glass down indignantly. "I did not lose your friendship ring! I lost some dumb ring you got out of a gum machine—"

"A gum machine! Gilbert Hill gave me that ring last year at the graduation dance."

"Gil Hill." She made a rude noise. "He's skinny and his hair looks as if he chews on it—how could you go out with him?"

I drew a breath. We got into it pretty well, dragging out things that were years old, examining minutely each other's bad habits and unbearable friends, barring no holds since no one was there to shut us up. We had brought things to a head and were simmering down again, she reminding me of the time I had allegedly pushed her off her tricycle at the tender age of four, and I pointing out that life would be simpler and more comfortable if she would not throw everything she owned on our bedroom floor, when I realized we were not alone. Someone was breathing behind me. Erica cut short whatever she was saying, her face breaking into a little shame-faced grin.

I turned slowly. Neil, who was used to us, said mildly, "I rang the doorbell, but you didn't hear. I came to pick up Brian."

I felt like kicking the refrigerator. I felt like throwing the casserole at the ceiling. Every time he was around, some member of my family got me tangled in a stupid, childish argument. It was a conspiracy. I went to the sink and started jabbing burned pieces of casserole out of the dish.

"Brian's in his room," I said shortly. I heard him leave the kitchen. Then I felt my stomach waver as if it had turned to water and fish were jumping in it. I wanted to cry, but Erica was haunting the room. She was making a peanut butter sandwich. She didn't say anything, which surprised me. I couldn't tell whether she was being merciful or just prudent. The phone rang, and she answered it. She handed the receiver to me, her face carefully neutral, and I realized suddenly what it was. She liked Neil, too, and she had also been a little embarrassed. That made me feel better. It was not complete victory, then, but a sort of stalemate.

Barbara said, "Joslyn?"

"Hi." I cleared my throat. "What's up?"

"You sound funny."

"I was just—swallowing something."

"Oh. Can you meet me at that house at about eight-thirty? Bring a flashlight."

"Sure."

"Did you read *The Scarlet Letter* yet?"

"Oh, Barbara—"

"Go read it." Her voice faded a little at a babble in the background. "Kim and Sara, stop that! Go outside if you want to play Ping-Pong. Joslyn? I have to stay with the twins until my mother gets home from shopping, but I'll meet you after that. Okay?"

"Okay."

I hung up glumly. For some reason, the prospect of exploring a dirty old house did not appeal to me at the moment, nor did reading *The Scarlet Letter*. Erica had gone, leaving the bread and peanut butter open on the cupboard. I made myself a sandwich and ate it moodily. I wanted to go to Neil's party. I wanted to dress in my best pair of faded jeans, and my eyelet lace smock with the deep neckline and the sash. I would wear pale blue eye shadow, and comb my hair until it was smooth as the underside of a shell. Then, when Neil saw me, all memory of the girl squabbling in the kitchen with Erica would fade from his mind and he would . . . he would . . . But I couldn't. Such was my despair that I actually got up and found *The Scarlet Letter* and read a few pages while I ate. It went down about as easily as the peanut butter.

When I got to the deserted house, Claudia was there, but Barbara hadn't shown up yet. It wasn't quite dark, but the sun had gone down, leaving a little trail of clouds like a flock of sheep wandering home. Claudia was nervous. She was shivering a little, even though the evening was warm, and she kept switching her flashlight on and off with her thumb. Finally I took it away from her.

"Will you stop that," I moaned. "Half a block from the police station, and a street full of nervous old ladies, and you have to do Morse code with your flashlight."

"I don't know Morse code," she said miserably.

"If you don't want to do this, don't. It's all right. Nobody will blame you."

"I want to." The streetlight went on suddenly over our heads, and she jumped. I pulled her into the shadows of the yard. Standing behind the pine trees, it was dark and secret; the house at our backs, with its broken window staring at us like a black eyeball, made even me nervous. It was soundless and ugly. The street itself, usually friendly with flowers and children and ancient, colorful cars, was suddenly alien seen from the other side of the pine. I felt Claudia's fingers close, cold, on my arm.

"Maybe there's a mad woman living in it," she whispered. "Like in *Jane Eyre*. Or a ghost—that's why it's deserted: there's a ghost bewailing its sins on earth—"

"I don't hear any bewailing," I said crossly.

"In this movie I saw, the mad woman was chained in a deserted windmill, and when she crept up behind you, you could hear her chain rustling along the wood floor, and that's the last sound you ever heard, because she strangled you with her chain."

"Claudia!" But it was too late; I could feel the blood prickling all over me. Then, staring back at the broken window with the darkness inside outlined by silvery shards of glass, I saw Joe Takaota, with his quiet face and dark hair, come to stand looking out at the dirt and dark pines. He pushed his hands suddenly through the broken glass, cutting his wrists. I blinked. He faded back into the darkness, and I took a step forward as if to follow him, because I didn't want him to be alone in the darkness. Claudia said, "There's Barbara."

We hissed at her from the yard. I saw her quick glance up and down the street, and then she slid between the pine boughs and joined us. I could see her eyes gleam in the darkness.

"I'm sorry I'm late," she said. "My mother thinks I'm at the library."

"So does mine," Claudia said surprisedly. That made me giggle.

"They're going to wonder why it's suddenly such a popular place. Should we go through the front door or try a window?"

The windows were nailed shut, so we went through the front door. It took a little work, and what we did would come definitely under the heading of breaking and entering. Once inside, we took deep breaths of relief. Claudia switched on her light, which I had stupidly given back to her, and we pounced on it, squealing, "No! Someone will see it through the windows!"

"What are we going to do, then?" she demanded. "We have to see."

"You can see a little," Barbara said. "Let your eyes get used to it. We'll use the lights only if we have to."

Light from the street made a pale circle through one of the windows, enough for us to see a small, bare living room with a ruined fireplace. Some of the bricks from it lay on the floor; a beer can gleamed in a corner. I said, surprised, "People have been in here. Look at all the papers." There were sandwich bags and old newspapers scattered on the floor. As I looked at them, something ran squealing through the mess. I felt a chill glide through me from head to foot. I clutched Claudia, whispering faintly.

"Rats."

"A rat," Barbara said firmly, and Claudia, in a voice shaken but staunch, backed her up.

"Rat. Singular."

Two against one. I let go of Claudia, swallowing my singular horror. We went into the kitchen. The window was boarded up there, so we flashed one light carefully. There were sagging cupboards, a rusty sink, and a pipe coming down where the stove had been, drifted with cobwebs like grey white smoke. None of us wanted to go into the bathroom; Barbara finally gave it one quick sweep of light to see that there were no dead bodies or colonies of rats in it. She said surprisedly, "There's nothing in it. The toilet's gone. There's nothing left but a few water pipes."

"Maybe that's to keep people from coming in and using it," Claudia suggested.

"Maybe." Barbara opened the last door. There was only one bedroom, the house was that small. The windows in that room were boarded up, so she closed the door behind us and we switched on the flashlights. The room was square, with a single closet whose door had long since disappeared. The floor was clean but dusty. Big fuzzballs drifted where we walked; pieces of torn wallpaper hung off the walls, showing older wallpaper and plaster beneath. It was motionless. Standing in the silence of it, I felt a sadness gnaw at the back of my mind, like an itch I couldn't scratch. Being in the musty, empty room made me feel that no one would ever love me, and nothing worth even moving my mouth to talk about would ever happen to me again. Barbara moved to the center of the room, let her light glide over the walls. It slid across the ceiling, and she made a little sound.

"Look at that."

There was a wide skylight above our heads, locked, dusty, and streaked, but not boarded. In the light we could make out, very faintly, patterns of pine branches pressing against it from a tree. I think it was the skylight and the tree beyond it that decided Barbara. She drew one breath, and another. Then she said, "We could paint the walls. Landscapes and big streaks of color. Orange, blue, purple—"

"Plants," Claudia said. Her voice honked a little. "And flowers."

"Masses of flowers, yes. And a tree. A tree that grew out of a mountain. Shells from the sea. And fish. Starfish. Sea horses."

"Light—lots of light. Candles, and old-fashioned lamps—"

"A rocking chair—"

"A sheepskin rug—"

"Flutes—he loved flutes, and recorders, wood, ceramic—"

"Mobiles. And glass prisms, to catch the light."

"Wind chimes. Tapestries—"

"And bells, and—"

"Big, bright velvet pillows—"

"And books."

That stopped Barbara a moment. Then she said, "Yes. He loved science fiction. We'll paint a space ship on the walls—a galaxy—" She looked at me suddenly, the light running like a hand between us, and I could see her smiling, more excited than I could remember her for a long time. "What do you think?"

They had caught me up in their excitement. The room was half-beautiful already with their words. I laughed.

"We've only got a few weeks. We'd better get started."

"Tomorrow," Barbara said. "I want to get a tree from Big Basin. Can you come?"

I drew a breath, thinking rapidly. "Yes."

"How will we get up there?" Claudia said. "Our parents won't let us go alone. We can't camp alone without permission."

"We can bike up. People are always—"

"Thirty miles," I breathed. "Uphill."

"It's not uphill all the way. After the summit, you go down. You can coast. Is it all right?" she pleaded. "We could make it back the same day."

"Maybe," I said doubtfully.

"I'll go alone. Joe loved that place. He hiked all the trails in it, even the long one to the sea. He loved the giant redwoods. I can go alone."

"No," said Claudia.

"No," I said grimly. Biking thirty miles uphill was little compared to what I knew I had to do before morning. "I'm coming, too. I hope."

I finished *The Scarlet Letter* at four o'clock in the morning. Erica, who had wakened three times to beg me to shut off the light, didn't even move as I dropped the book and the notes for my report on the floor, and my face on the pillow. My impressions of the book were that I knew more than I ever cared to know about Hester and her love affair, but I did have the makings of the best book report I had ever given in my life, with all kinds of references to symbolism, which Mr. Frank loved. I barely had the strength to lift one arm to turn off the light.

I reported to breakfast at eight with dark circles under my eyes and my book report notes in hand. My parents, who were barely awake themselves over their coffee, were startled to see me.

"Hello," I said, dragging myself to a chair. "Did you have a good time last night?"

"We had a very nice time," my father said. "What in the world did you do all night?"

"I studied." I pushed the notes in front of him and put my head down on my arms. "Does coffee really help?"

My mother handed me her cup. "How come you stayed up so late? What are you—" She stopped. She knew me pretty well. I took a sip of her coffee. As usual, it tasted terrible, but it woke my mouth up. My father, who read engineering magazines and an occasional *Playboy,* was staring at my notes a little blankly. I took a breath.

"You see, that's all the homework I have this weekend. It's all done. And I wanted to take a bike ride with Barbara this morning. If that's okay." I felt my father looking at me. My mother said, "Where to?"

"Out Saratoga Avenue. It's just pretty out there, and she wanted to go." Saratoga Avenue ran straight into the hills to Big Basin. I picked up the coffee cup again to hide the fact that I was holding my breath. My father smoothed down his hair.

"Well." I could tell he was nonplussed. He didn't like to countermand a direct order. I raised my eyes to his face.

"Please," I begged. "I stayed up till four in the morning just to do this. I studied all night, and everything is done, and it's going to be the best book report I've ever given."

He looked at my mother. She shrugged a little, so he said, "All right. But if you get anything lower than a B on that report, you're grounded until the end of the year."

I sighed in relief. "I won't. This report will be great. Thanks, Dad." I gave my mother back her coffee. "Thanks, Mom." I stood up blearily, and she said, "Where are you going?"

"To get dressed."

"Well, for heaven's sake, have some breakfast." She got up and began rattling pans. "You'll wear yourself out."

So I rode over to Barbara's with a load of bacon and eggs in my stomach, which, after four hours' sleep, was barely awake to cope with it. I had thought the night before that *The Scarlet Letter* was bad, but that bicycle ride was a nightmare. We did fine riding through town with the road wide and flat to the edge of the hills, but the moment we got to Saratoga, we started winding uphill. I was sick twice before we reached the summit in the early afternoon.

Going downhill, on the skinny little road leading into the park, it was beautiful. We were exhausted from the ride up, which we took partly on foot, after dodging cars, breathing car fumes, sweating and burning in the hot morning and barely managing to pedal. Coasting down under the flick of shadows, we began to feel better. Redwoods, curly oak, and the strange green and orange trees that split out of their bark like molting lizards surrounded us, peaceful and still. The air smelled of warm earth, old leaves, and moss. The road was old and patched; it wandered around corners, dodging huge redwoods, wiggling like a brook, the kind of road that when you see it out of a car window, makes you wonder where it goes. This one led us an hour later to the park headquarters and food.

We bought hamburgers at the snack bar and sat on the big redwood steps in front of the gift shop, our bikes lying at our feet. There were people everywhere, camping, picnicking, and just wandering around looking at the deer and the trees. The redwoods, I knew vaguely, had been rescued from loggers around the turn of the century, and, after much legal wrangling, had been preserved for posterity by the government. Some of the trees were over two thousand years old, their insides scarred by fires, their trunks overgrown with boles like huge, knobby warts. Indians living in the area had never touched them, feeling that the deep, quiet basin of massive trees was sacred. The trees were sacred also to the forest rangers abounding in the park, who would take a dim view if they caught us stealing a tree under their noses.

I finished my hamburger and leaned back on the steps with a sigh. Barbara licked ketchup off her fingers.

"Do you feel better?" she said to me, and I nodded. The sun was toasting my feet beyond the edge of shadow I sat in, and everything was making me sleepy. I stretched.

"I want to find a nice tree and take a nap under it. It's so warm and peaceful."

"Me, too," Claudia said. She dropped her head on her arms. "I'm so sore from riding I don't know how I'm going to make it back."

"I could call my mother to get us," Barbara said, but Claudia shook her head.

"You'd have to tell her what we're doing up here, and why you stole a tree. I don't think," she added heavily after a moment, "we should get caught doing that. There's a whopping fine."

The legal mind. I said, "For one little tree? I can imagine explaining that to my dad."

But Barbara only said decisively, "We won't get caught." She stood up, and Claudia groaned. She sat down again, smiling. "All right. I'm tired, too. Let's go take a nap. But just a short one."

We rode down one of the roads in the picnic area and found an empty table beside a creek. Claudia and Barbara collapsed under the shadow of a redwood; I climbed on top of the picnic table and lay down. High above me, three trees converged, balancing the sun on their heads. A warm breeze rustled across my stomach; an acorn thumped to the ground in its wake. The creek made funny little noises, like a baby talking to itself while it played with its toes. Blue jays squabbled in the distance, and I heard something with tiny claws skitter up a trunk behind me. I closed my eyes.

I woke up to someone saying my name. Barbara stood over me, leaves and pine needles in her hair. I sat up. The air was a different color, a sort of smoky blue, with long, blinding shafts of sunlight pouring between the trees. My voice croaked.

"What time is it?"

"I don't know," Barbara said. "But it's late. We have to hurry."

I got down from the table stiffly. I could smell campfires, whiffs of other people's suppers. Claudia, brushing things out of her hair, looking wider awake than either of us, said, "I'm supposed to go to my aunt's house for supper tonight."

Barbara covered her eyes with her hands. "I'm supposed to—oh, well. We'll just tell them what happened—except for the tree. The tree." She looked around vaguely. I said hastily, "You can't just dig one up and ride with it in your bike basket through the park headquarters."

"I know. I was going to take one of his favorite trails and get one, but it's so late . . . Meteor Trail."

"Meteor," Claudia whispered, staring in front of her as if she could see a golden shower of them falling through the trees. Barbara nodded sleepily.

"It follows Opal Creek; the water is pink and gold in places there, and the banks are soft and green with moss. One of the pioneers settled there; Joe used to try and figure out where his house was."

Claudia looked at me suddenly. She didn't have to say anything. I grinned. "I don't care. The sooner I go home, the sooner I catch hell. I might as well stay here all night."

"We'll hurry," Barbara said absently.

But we didn't. We left our bikes half-sheltered in a huge hollow tree and found the beginning of the trail not far away. The sun had gone behind a mountain; the trees were absolutely soundless. Moving through the grey green twilight, the trees rising round and still as pillars in a church, I felt as though we were in a different world, where little things like being home late couldn't matter. The sounds from the campers faded behind us as we followed the creek. I realized slowly that the forest probably hadn't changed much since Indians had looked at the same trees I looked at. The trees might have grown a few feet; a few more leaves had decayed, and a few more had fallen, but that was about it. And we were walking, for some reason, as quietly as they must have walked, our footsteps soft and careful on the thick needles.

"How," I asked after a while, "could anyone have built a house here? It's too steep." There weren't many level spots on the trail, and we were all puffing a little.

"I don't know," Barbara said. "But they say he lived here nearly a hundred years ago. He ate fish from the stream and berries. And he built his house and brought his wife here from Ireland after a while. They lived alone for years, and they were very poor. I read once he had some horses pastured for the winter in a meadow higher up, and when spring came, he went to get them and found that grizzly bears had eaten them."

Something caught in my throat. "Grizzly bears?"

She turned to look back at me, grinning. "There haven't been grizzly bears in California for almost a hundred years. I made sure of that the first time I came up here."

"I'm glad." I thought of the woman coming from, perhaps, a little village in Ireland to live in this odd place tucked away in the mountains, when the cities I knew were just growing up all around them, not far away. I wondered what she was like: if she dreamed of Ireland and hated the mosquitoes and bears, or if she shot wild cats with a fearless hand and opened the doors of her house at evening to watch the stars come out.

Barbara put her hand out suddenly to stop me, startling me. She whispered, "There."

In the center of a rare bit of level ground on the other side of the creek, just the right size to hold a one-room cabin, stood a tiny tree. It was about two feet high, beautifully symmetrical, like a young green flame against the dark forest. It drew Barbara like a moth off the trail to clamber over the flotsam and jetsam that had built up around the creek: old branches, brambles, tree trunks. We followed more slowly. Claudia, never at her best when balancing on tree trunks, gave up completely and sat down to wait for us. I thrashed across some old dry branches and joined Barbara. She was already on her knees, digging with her hands in the soft earth.

"Smell it," she said, and I sniffed. It was soft and perfect, with delicate green webs instead of needles. I sank my hands in the bracken around it and immediately disturbed a family of roly-poly bugs. They all curled up into little grey balls, their heads in their stomachs. I poked them out of the way. Barbara, her face flushed, stopped working to watch. She brushed hair out of her face, leaving a streak behind.

"We have to hide it."

"We have to get it out first," I said. It was a stubborn little tree. I had a sudden image of its roots spreading out underneath us through the whole of the park. A daddy longlegs climbed huffily out of the hole I had made, and I waited respectfully for it to get out of my way. All that insect life was making me nervous, but Barbara was ploughing away, ignoring nonessentials.

"We have to hide it," she said again, and I had a brainstorm.

"There are garbage bins all over the park. There must be a box or a bag in one of them."

She flashed a smile at me, her face easing again. "He'll like it. Joslyn, isn't it beautiful? I love it. Only it's so damn stubborn."

I said, "It's gorgeous. Do you know what? I just realized why they call this Meteor Trail."

"Why?"

"Look."

The stream, cutting between the trees, slit a jagged strip of their thick branches open to the darkening sky, and stars by the hundreds were shooting down at us. Barbara's mouth opened.

"Oh, Joslyn," she whispered. "I didn't know it was so late." Across the stream Claudia sat hugging her knees and staring upward. A frog grunted somewhere in the dark stream, and her face turned towards it. She said, "Barbara—"

"I know. We'll hurry."

The tree finally came out. Barbara carried it in her arms like a baby across the stream, while I scooped dirt back into the hole and scattered leaves across it so the rangers wouldn't be upset. Crossing the stream, my foot crashed through a net of branches, nearly hitting the water, and the frogs gave me a whole chorus of nervous noises. We went as fast as we could down the trail, but the whole world turned pitch black before we ever reached the bottom. The only thing that kept us on the trail was the stream, glimmering every once in awhile in faint, knife-thin strokes of light.

No one spoke. As safe as I knew that park was, I was frightened of its silence, and of the darkness that had welled over it so deeply we couldn't even see each other's eyes. I followed Barbara's panting, and thought of the Irish woman, so far from people, so far from the sounds of people in that night. She lived in a world of rules different from people's rules, and I had a sudden feeling that neither she nor I belonged there in that black silence. Maybe the Indians had been right.

The stars above us spilled out suddenly, like a stream spills into a river. Something thumped under our feet, and Claudia's breath left her in a gasp.

"The bridge, I remember. I know where we are. There's the road—"

It looked like a faint, grey river, so faint we could barely see it. I stepped off the bridge in relief, and fell into space.

It ended so soon I barely had time to cry out. My arms were raw from scraping against dirt, and I had somehow knocked the breath out of myself. I heard Barbara's voice.

"Joslyn? Where are you?"

"I don't know." My voice was whimpering because I couldn't get any air for a minute. Then I realized what happened. "I fell in the ditch by the road."

"Can you get out?" I felt a hand brush over my face. "Joslyn, say something."

"Of course I can get out. I'm just tired." Barbara's hand found my wrist. I pulled myself out, and she helped me to my feet.

"Are you all right? Are you hurt?" I could feel her close to me, but I couldn't see her. I could smell the tree, though, as I brushed the dirt off my arms and the front of my shirt. The fall had disoriented me.

"Where do we go from here? I don't remember. How are we going to find our bikes?"

"They're just down the road a little," Claudia said. "Remember? We went up the road coming to the trail; now we go down."

Facing the right direction on the road, I saw a familiar yellow light. I said tiredly, "And there, thank God, is a bathroom."

Seeing each other, at last, in the bathroom light made us laugh, because we looked exactly like people would look after they had just stolen a tree with their bare hands. We washed and picked all the dead things out of our hair, then went rummaging through the trash bin for a box. The campers were quiet; their lanterns hung like stars among the trees. In the restless wash of their fires, the huge trees loomed quiet, changeless, blurring into the night. With the noise we made, we must have sounded like raccoons grubbing for food, and we brought one noisy dog out of bed to get yelled at by his owner. We emptied a couple of grocery bags, and put the bottom of the tree in one, and the other over the top, so it was completely hidden. It looked suspicious, but gave no evidence of what it might be. The ranger truck, passing us on the road as we went to get our bikes, flared its lights over us and went on without stopping.

We retrieved our bikes, and Barbara put the tree in her basket. Then we stood on the road and looked at each other in the dark. Someone drew a breath; it was Barbara.

"I'll call my mother."

I drew a breath and held it for a moment. Then my tongue said reluctantly, "Call her and tell her where you are. But we've got three bikes. I'll ask my dad to bring the station wagon."

"I'm sorry," Barbara said helplessly. "I got you all into this. I wish we had sleeping bags to spend the night."

"So do I." I would have preferred facing my parents in the daylight after giving them a night to cool off.

Claudia said surprisingly, "I don't care. They make us do enough difficult things, like going to school every day. We deserve this. Sometimes I like to talk during the day."

I tried to see her face, but all I could see was a black blob. I said, "You're absolutely right. That's exactly what I'll tell my dad."

But, calling from the phone booth at the ranger station, all I got was Brian. He whooped into my ear, "Where have you been!"

"Don't shout. I want to talk to Mom."

"Where are you? Mom's not here. They're over at Barbara's house—where are you? Did you get picked up for something?"

"Yes," I said wearily. "I'm at Juvenile Hall being booked for prostitution."

For once I caught him wordless. His voice changed. "Come on. They thought—we thought you might have gotten wrapped around a truck or something. Dad called the police, and Mom's been calling hospitals."

A lump rose like a fish in my throat. "Brian," I said, pleading for mercy, "we biked up to Big Basin; we're fine—"

"Well, why the hell didn't you call?"

"I didn't think— Shut up and listen. Please. Call Mrs. Takaota's and Mrs. Gill's—the numbers are on the list by the phone—and tell them we're all right. And will you—will you tell Dad we need a ride home? We've got our bikes and it's dark."

He was silent again; I heard his breathing. "You're incredible. You want me to tell Dad that?"

"Please."

"It's your skin. If I were you, I'd take a long hike or something."

"Brian!"

"All right, all right—" He said something to someone with him, and I heard a laugh. "I'll tell everyone. Wait at the ranger station and don't move. See you later. Don't worry," he added unexpectedly, before he hung up, and it helped a little. I sat down with Barbara and Claudia on the steps in front of the office, where the porch light was shining, and told them. Barbara whispered, "Hospitals."

"I don't care," Claudia said stubbornly, and oddly enough, I didn't care too much either. We had accomplished what we came for, and we still had a lot to do. I just hoped that my dad would refrain from grounding me for six months. I said, "What should we do next?" and a ranger said behind us, "Are those your bikes over there, girls?"

Something came then and breathed the breath back out of my mouth. We turned slowly. He stood above us on the steps, eight feet tall, with enormous bulbous eyes that held ours steadily. Barbara said, her voice small and soft, "Yes."

"Well, could you move them, please? They're blocking my truck, and I want to go home to bed."

He changed suddenly, turned into a shortish, lean man with his hat pushed wearily back on his head. We scrambled to our feet eagerly.

He said, "You can put them here by the porch."

"That's okay," Barbara said. "We'll put them over there

in the parking lot." We jumped off the porch before he could speak again, and he stood and watched us while we moved the bikes across the road into the shadows. When we came back, he said, a little puzzled, "Are you girls camping here? You're a little young to be up here by yourselves."

"No," Barbara said. "We rode up here this morning, and we're waiting for our parents to give us a ride home."

He chuckled. "Good thinking. That's quite a ride. It's too bad you didn't plan to stay."

She sighed. "We didn't plan anything right."

"Well. If you run into any problems, just tell the ranger in the office. I'm going to bed. Good night."

We watched him drive off. Somebody had to say it eventually, so I said it. "The only problem is: I'm starving to death."

"Try not to think about it," Claudia said listlessly.

It was a long wait. The place was dead silent but for insects tinking against the porch light, and the occasional rustle of a deer or raccoon or something nameless off to its private business. Rangers in their trucks passed every once in a while, patrolling; and every time we saw their lights coming toward us we sat up a little, and when they passed, we settled back into ourselves. I got tired of sitting on the steps, so I went across the road and sat on the fence that enclosed a little clearing for the deer. A couple of them lifted their heads out of the long grass; I saw their soft, dark eyes and tiered antlers. Beyond the porchlight I could see the stars, tiny, ice white specks following their own rules far above the trees. Staring up at them, I had a funny feeling inside me, maybe because I was so hungry. But I thought suddenly that all the familiar things around me: the deer, the trees, the raccoons, Barbara, and Claudia, were as strange and unexpected as the stars. Nothing was familiar anymore; the things I had taken for granted, even laughed at, like the raccoons with their masks and child's hands, were really amazing, incredible shapes to appear on the planet whirling underneath me in the middle of nowhere. I looked at Barbara sitting under the light, with her thick, dark hair falling to her waist, and suddenly I knew her and didn't know her. I even felt strange inside my own skin, as if I had never realized before that I existed. It was a weird feeling. I came out of it slowly, seeing lights again, and catching, as I moved my hand on the rail, a sliver of wood in my palm. I squinted down at it, picking at it by the vague light. The truck paused, idling in the road. A voice said, "Joslyn?"

It was Neil.

He said, getting out, "I was with Brian when you called. I had the truck with me, so I thought I'd save your parents a trip." He smiled as Claudia and Barbara came to join us. "Ready to go home?"

Coming unexpectedly like that out of the darkness, he looked nameless for a second, and I gawked at him before I slid off the fence. Then I realized who he was, and that he'd come all the way up a mountain to rescue us, looking as calm and self-sufficient as if we'd been just down the street. Something in my throat wanted to laugh suddenly, happily, for no reason, but I squashed it.

"Do you— I can't remember if you've met Barbara."

"Once," Barbara said a little shyly. "At your house, Joslyn." Claudia, hovering uneasily behind her, shocked us both by saying to Neil out loud, her voice wobbling a little, "Did Brian call my parents?"

He nodded. "Your dad was going to come and get you, but Brian told your mother I would. Where are your bikes?"

"Right here," Barbara said. She lifted hers up, to heave it over the side of the truck, I suppose, but he took it from her.

"I'll get it." He opened the tailgate and lifted it up. He stubbed the front wheel of the bike on the tailgate, and the bag bounced out at his feet. He reached down for it. Then his head lifted, and his eyes went to Barbara's face.

She put a finger over her mouth. He looked away from her, shifted the tree to the side of the truck, and laid the bike flat. We wheeled the others over and he settled them to his liking. Then he jumped down and closed the gate.

He eyed us briefly, and said, "You're all thin, we can fit in front."

Barbara, who I thought was too preoccupied to think of such things, stepped aside and let me go in first to sit beside him. We were quiet while he backed the truck up and turned it around. I watched his hands on the wheel, lean, the fingers square-tipped; he lifted one hand to brush at the hair falling forward into his eyes, and the fish in my stomach jumped up suddenly, dove deep. Then my stomach made a noise, and he grinned at me.

"Hungry?"

I drew a breath. "Starving!" I settled back in the seat. "We ate lunch, then fell asleep for hours, then hiked up Meteor Trail without any supper—"

"Is that where you got the tree?"

"Yeah. We carried it down the mountain in the dark. It was weird; it's not like city darkness; it's a different kind. It's black."

He glanced at me. "Is that why you rode up? For a tree?"

I nodded. I wanted to tell him, to trust him, because I knew he would understand. But it was Barbara's idea and Barbara's tree. And she was quiet beside me. Claudia, too shy to talk now, tilted her head against the window and closed her eyes. Neil switched on the radio, fiddled with the knob, trying to find some music.

"We could stop for hamburgers at Boulder Creek."

Barbara said suddenly, "Neil—" Her voice stuck. He turned the radio off, finding nothing but static, and for some reason it seemed darker. Then his head turned.

"I'm sorry—"

She wiggled a little against me. "Nothing. It's just that—the tree is for Joe."

We both looked at her, me the longest since he had to jerk the truck out of the way of a tree. He said softly, "Is Joe coming home?"

"Yes. That's why we came up here to get a tree. Because he loved—he loved it here."

"Oh." His voice was soft in the darkness. He glanced toward her again. "How is he?"

"I don't know. I haven't— I haven't seen him for so long. But that's why we stole the tree. I thought he might like it."

"You rode all the way up here just to do that?"

"Yes," she said tiredly. "It had to be a certain tree."

"I guess so. When is he coming?"

"Next month some time."

"That's good. I'd like to see him again."

She nodded. "The twins really miss him."

"It must have been hard to try to explain what happened to them."

"It was. My mother said he was sick, and he had to go away for a while to get well. They were always wanting to visit him, asking when he was going to come home when she—when even she didn't know." Her face was bent, hidden behind her hair. I was surprised to hear her talk about those things to someone who was almost a stranger, but then Neil was easy to talk to. She lifted her face suddenly, shook her hair back. "It was really nice of you to come and get us."

"Well. Mr. and Mrs. Carter spent half the day worrying, and they were tired, and anyway, I didn't have much else to do."

"Was—were they very angry?" I asked cautiously. He shook his head.

"They were relieved."

"Wait'll they have a chance to think about it," I muttered, and he smiled.

"Just explain."

"I'm not about to tell them I rode up here to steal a tree."

"Then how are you going to explain the tree?" he asked practically. We were silent, then. Barbara shifted again. She drew a breath, then another, and I knew what was just about to come out. I knew Neil was nice, but she didn't know him well, and I was surprised.

"There's a little— There's a little deserted house on Briar Avenue. Could you stop there for a moment while we put the tree in it?"

He almost stopped the truck. "Barbara," he said, and for some reason, when he said her name, it sounded unfamiliar, as though it belonged to someone I didn't know. "Haven't you broken enough laws for one day? Besides, you should replant it."

"Well, I can't take it home. It's for Joe."

"But Joe—" he said, bewildered; and she broke in.

"We're making a place for him in that house. A place for him to go when he—instead of having to try to kill himself. A private, beautiful place."

This time he did stop. Claudia lifted her head, blinking. The engine idled softly in the darkness; his face was dark, as he half-turned himself to look at her. He said after a moment, "Oh." It was almost a whisper. Then he cleared his throat and started the truck again. "Oh. Well. Do you want me to keep it for you?"

Barbara leaned her head back against the seat and said, as if she had expected Neil to say that, "I'll come and get it tomorrow. If you could—if you could just put it in some water . . . I hope it's all right."

"Trees are tough."

"But this one is only a baby. It had to be a special tree," she added again, her voice scratching, and he said, "I know how to take care of a tree. What—how are you going to do this?"

"We'll do it," she just said. He nodded.

"I believe it."

We stopped for hamburgers at the nearest town, and pulled into Mrs. Takaota's driveway an hour later. She came out with both the twins to watch Neil take Barbara's bike out. Sara said cheerfully to us, "You're in trouble."

"I know," Barbara said, climbing out. "Thanks, Neil." She looked at her mother. "I'm sorry."

Mrs. Takaota, shaking her head, smiled suddenly. I envied Barbara, as we backed out to go to Claudia's, for having such a reasonable mother.

Mr. Gill kept saying, as Neil handed down Claudia's bike, "You rode thirty miles up the mountain? All that way? Thirty miles?"

"We walked some of it," Claudia said modestly, but I heard the sudden pride in her voice. She waved good-bye to us, and I was alone in the silence with Neil.

I was almost too tired and too content to talk. In the flick of street lights, Neil's hair was melded smooth; his face beneath it was shadowed. He turned to me suddenly, as if he had felt me looking at him, and I said, "Did you have a good party Friday night?"

"Pretty good." He stopped for a red light. "How did you— What made Barbara think of an idea like that?"

"I don't know. We were just talking, and it sounded like a good idea. She just didn't want Joe ever to do that again."

"Do you think you can stop him? She thinks so. Do you?"

I hesitated. The little, weary room with its peeling wallpaper and boarded windows drifted into my mind. Staring at it, I said softly, "I don't care. If she thinks so, we can do it."

The light changed. The truck jerked a little as he switched gears. He was frowning. "I hope so. She— I hope so. I'll help."

My brows went up in surprise. Then I remembered that Joe had been in Neil's class. I said, "You realize all this is very illegal."

"That house has been empty for years. Besides, you don't seem very concerned about legality."

"Well, it's different for us."

"Why?"

"Because we—you—we aren't vice-president of the junior class, or on the basketball team. And we're not studying political science, either. We can always say we didn't know any better. You can't. What if you get thrown in jail? You'll get kicked off the basketball team."

"Ignorance of the law is no excuse. I'll just say I fell in with bad company."

"Neil—"

"Joslyn, that's silly. If we get caught, we'll just explain."

My eyebrows were getting tired up in the air, so I let them down. "I didn't know you were allowed to do that," I said doubtfully.

"Anyway, we won't get caught. Nobody cares about that house. You tell me what you want me to do, and I'll do it."

"Sure." I still felt a little dazed. "I didn't know you knew Joe that well."

"It's not—" The truck jerked again. "It's— Brian and Joe and I were freshmen together. This year, Brian dropped out on his birthday; and Joe— Joe just gave up. He—"

"Do you know why?" I whispered. "Do you know why?"

He shook his head. We were almost home. "Just living."

I didn't catch as much hell as I thought I would from my parents. I told them how we were seized with an impulse to ride up the mountain, didn't realize how long it would take, and fell asleep for four hours the minute we got there. My mother said, "You could have called sooner."

"I didn't think. I just didn't think."

"Typical," Brian grunted, and for once I was grateful. It was exactly the kind of stupid thing I would do without

premeditation. My father, drinking straight scotch, pinpointed me with his eyes.

"You—" he said. I waited, breathless.

"Yes, sir?"

He gave up and turned to my mother. "What are we going to do with this child?"

My mother shook her head. Brian suggested, "Put her back under her toadstool."

"Take her back for a refund," Erica said gleefully. "Throw her back and try again."

My mother's brows went up at that. "No, sir!"

So, swallowing my tongue and letting Erica and scotch handle matters, I got off pretty easily. I dragged myself to bed and slept until noon.

Sunday afternoon, sitting in the park and chewing grass stems, we had a serious consultation.

"We should make a list," Claudia said. "We should get organized."

"Were your parents mad?" I asked curiously, and she shook her head.

"No." She sounded still surprised about it. "They— I never do things like that. I never do anything. I think they liked it. Only—"

I nodded. "Next time, warn them first. Call when you get there. Plan ahead, get organized. Only how can you get organized when you don't know what you're doing in the first place? I suppose in some magical, mystical way you're supposed to know."

"We have to get the tree from Neil," Barbara said. She was stretched out on her side with her head on one hand. It was a beautiful afternoon, with a baby blue sky and grass bright as cellophane. Lying on my stomach, I dropped my face deep in the grass and daisies and sniffed. I felt something tickle my nose, and stared into the bulbous eyes of a big brown beetle. I got up fast, squealing. Claudia laughed until she had hiccups, and the beetle bumped along over the grass blades, ignoring us with dignity. I settled down again carefully. Then I said, "Oh, I forgot. Neil said he wants to help."

They gawked at me. "Neil Brown?" Barbara said, to make sure. "Neil?"

I nodded. "He said so last night, taking me home. Out of the blue. Is that okay?" I asked casually, and Claudia grinned.

Barbara said, "Joslyn, you're blushing. What else did he say last night?"

I sighed. "Nothing. He just wants to help. So of course I said yes. Is that okay?"

She nodded dazedly. "Of course. I guess so. But I don't understand why."

"Joe was in his class," Claudia said.

"Yes, but they weren't— But Neil—" She gave up, shaking her head. "He must have known Joe better than I thought."

"We have to make a list," Claudia said, "so we know what we're doing."

So we made a list. Mulling it over afterwards, Barbara said thoughtfully, "We have some paint in the garage, old half-empty cans nobody's used for ages."

"So do we," Claudia said.

"I have some wind chimes," I said, sucking on the pencil eraser. "One with little copper pipes, and one with painted glass . . . but the windows are boarded up; there's no wind, unless we can get the skylight open."

"Fan," Claudia suggested.

"No electricity."

There was a silence. Barbara said, "We'll try the skylight. I can make pillows; we've got a lot of scraps around the house from sewing."

"I have some burlap," I said. "I could make some banners—burlap and felt, to hang down from the ceiling."

"Good."

"Put it on the list," Claudia said. "Where are we going to get a sea horse?"

"Pet shop," Barbara said.

"But you'd need a fish tank, and a filter, and all kinds of—"

I straightened so fast I surprised myself. "Brian has a fish tank he hasn't used for years in the attic. Fish. They're bright—blue, red, orange—they'd be pretty."

"Put it on the list," Claudia said.

And Barbara said, "That's good. I really wanted a sea horse. What else?"

"Plants," I read. "Flowers. Candles, lamps, flutes, mobiles, tapestries, books, rocking chair, sheepskin rug and prisms. What on earth is a prism?"

"It's glass in a geometric shape," Claudia said. "Triangle, square, hexagon. You look through it, and it refracts light into neat colors."

"Oh." I swallowed the grass I was chewing and picked a new blade. "Well, where are we going to get prisms? And a rocking chair? Or a sheepskin rug? We're not exactly millionaires."

"Well," Barbara said reluctantly. "Maybe we can get along without the sheepskin and the prisms. But I really would like a rocking chair. I'll get it. I'll think of something. What else?"

I looked down at the list. "Candles are easy . . . flutes and recorders?"

Barbara's forehead wrinkled. "I'll find them. What—"

"Mobiles, they're easy. Books, easy. Tapestries."

"Well." She cleared her throat. "On some of these things we might have to compromise."

"First thing we have to do," Claudia said, "is clean that place up."

"Tonight," Barbara said. She lay back down on the grass. I smoothed the grass I had picked between my thumbs like a reed, and blew hard. A noise came out of it like the sound you might hear from an elephant blowing its nose. Barbara sat up again, fast, grinning.

"Joslyn—" Then her eyes went over my head. A shadow fell over me. She said shyly, "Hi, Neil."

I looked up. He was laughing down at me, his eyes the color of the warm sky. He gave Claudia, whose face had gone still, a polite nod, and waited to be invited before he sat. He said to Barbara, his face going a little red beneath his eyes as if he had suddenly, inexplicably, gone shy, too, "I went to your house; your mother said you should be here. I wanted to know what you want to do about the tree. I replanted it."

"You did?" she said wonderingly.

"I put it in a big ceramic pot. I hope— It's not a bad-looking pot." He shifted a little. "It's yellow."

Barbara, gazing up at him, closed her mouth finally. It was her secret, so she had to ask him to sit. "We were just—we were just talking about what we were going to put in the room. You can— Do you want to sit down? That was really nice of you to replant the tree."

"We were making a list," Claudia said abruptly, as if the words had been forced out of her, and her face went bright red. Sitting cross-legged between Barbara and me, Neil looked at her.

"Is it okay if I read it?" he asked, and at the uncertainty in his own voice, her face lost its tension. She stared at him, surprised.

"Sure." She took it off my knees and gave it to him.

He read it slowly, while we watched him, his head bent over the list, the wind straying through the hair on the back of his head. He finished it; his eyes went to Barbara's face.

"A sea horse?"

She flushed a little. "Well. Sea horses. I thought he might like one. I mean, how can you be depressed when you look at a sea horse?"

He smiled. "I guess not. You need a saltwater tank for that."

"We have Brian's old tank," I said. "Only I don't know how to set it up."

"You'd need electricity for a filter," he said, and I sighed.

"I forgot."

"Do we need a filter?" Barbara said pleadingly. "I'll change the water. I just have to know how much salt to put in it."

Neil glanced up from the list again. "I'll help you. I'll get you one."

We looked at him, amazed. He looked a little amazed, too, as if he hadn't expected himself to say that. Then he said abruptly, "Did you know that male sea horses carry their young in what looks like their stomach, and when they're born, the front part opens and the baby sea horses come out perfectly formed, tiny miniatures?"

Barbara, her mouth open again, smiled slowly. I got a sudden vision of a father sea horse rocking sedately in the middle of the ocean with his tummy open, and tiny, perfect sea horses, grave as gentlemen, drifting out of him like thoughts. Neil's face, lowered again to read, was pink, as if sitting among three girls and discussing the reproductive habits of sea horses was too much for him. I lay back down on the grass, my face in his shadow. I could hear his soft breathing.

Barbara, suddenly practical, said cautiously, "How much would it cost? I don't have much money."

"Oh . . ." He didn't look up. "Shouldn't be more than—a couple of dollars . . ."

She sighed with relief. "Good. That's so good. But Neil, you don't have to—I mean, you must have so many other things to do."

He came out from behind the list finally. "It's no problem. I like sea horses." He looked at me, smiling again. "Will Brian mind if we use his tank?"

I smiled back. "No. He hasn't used it for years."

"Well, I'll ask him if I can borrow it; that way he won't ask you a lot of questions." He went back to the list, leaving me breathless at his tact. "Prisms?"

"That's to look at light through," Barbara said, and I thought of something else. I sat up.

"There's no light! He has to come there at night. There's no wind for the wind chimes, no electricity for the fish, no light for the prisms—"

"Candles," Barbara said. Her hands had closed. "We will have candles. And oil lamps with colored oil; they're not expensive. We'll have light. And the movement of the air around the flames will stir the chimes. We'll have problems with this, but I know we can solve them. And it will work."

In spite of her words, I heard a faint shake of uncertainty in her voice. So I lied firmly, "We'll make it work. Only first we'd better get that place cleaned up. You want to do that tonight?"

She nodded. "If you're not too tired."

"Not a bit. What should we bring?"

"Brooms, rags, mops—"

"There's no water," Claudia said softly. Barbara dropped her face in her hands briefly. She said, emerging, "We'll just need a couple of buckets."

I grinned. "Are we going to ride to the front door of that place with brooms and buckets hanging from our bicycles? We'll look like chimney sweeps."

"Yes," Barbara said stubbornly. Neil cleared his throat.

"I have an idea. I want to bring that tree to the house tonight. So I can take you there in the truck, but we'll have to be careful going in. Is that okay?"

Barbara's eyes flicked to his face. They dropped again almost as fast. She said softly, "All right."

So we cleaned that evening. Neil picked me up first, promising my amazed parents and an equally amazed Brian that he would bring me home before curfew. And for two hours I watched him wielding a mop, wiping his wet hands over his face when he got tired, poking a broom at cobwebs in corners. It was so strange having him unexpectedly close that I almost couldn't talk, so for awhile, with Claudia shy again, only he and Barbara talked as they scrubbed the windows clean. Then, noticing my silence, he threw a damp cloth at me across the room, surprising me while I was tearing off the trailing ends of wallpaper. I soaked it and threw it back, hitting him in the chest, and he laughed. I tensed myself for the return attack, suddenly sprung tight, ready, longing for a rowdy, exuberant water fight. But he went back to work then, hard, his forehead wrinkling above his eyes as he concentrated. We finished with ten minutes to spare.

It didn't make the room any less sad-looking, but it was clean. Barbara swallowed a yawn.

"Now we can paint." The whole front of her blouse was wet; her jeans looked as if she had waded through a flood.

Claudia said blearily, "When?"

Neil, holding his mop like a musket, said, "Wednesday I can borrow the pickup again. And I don't have anything special to do."

Barbara's hand strayed to her hair. "Neil—"

"I want to do this," he said. "I want to." He met her eyes stubbornly; she looked down and said simply, "Okay. Thanks. Is Wednesday all right?" she asked Claudia and me. We nodded.

I remembered, mid-yawn, that I had a book report due the next day. I said tiredly, "Damn."

"What?" Barbara said.

"Oh, nothing. It's been a nice weekend."

"I know." She bent then, and tugged the tree that we had left in the hall into the center of the room. It was so green and alive against the torn walls that it made me smile. I felt Barbara's fingers close suddenly, tightly, on my arm as she stared down at it.

"We'll do it," she whispered, as though for the first time she believed it herself. "Joslyn, we're going to do it . . ."

I gave my oral report the next day in English. I talked about references to the color red in the book, and the cowardice of the Reverend Mr. Dimmesdale, and how all the women in the village probably secretly envied Hester for having a love affair and a child out of wedlock. I talked longer than I realized, since more came out of me than I thought I knew, and I was still going when the bell rang. Mr. Frank gave me a funny look. He crooked a finger, and when I went to his desk, he showed me the scarlet A he had given me in his grade book.

He said slowly, "You have brains. I thought they were there, but I was never sure."

"I wasn't either," I admitted.

He closed his grade book and asked hopefully, "What inspired you? Was it Hawthorne?"

I stared at him. He had to be kidding. "It was my father."

At home, I found my mother and Brian talking in the kitchen. I heard her say as I dropped my books on the living room couch, "I wish you would go back to school. I really do."

"It wouldn't work," Brian said softly. "I'd just cut classes like I did before. I'd never study. I just— I just can't get inspired."

"But it's not good for you to hang around the house doing nothing."

"I'll get a job and move out, then. Neil Brown says he can get me a job at the doughnut shop where he works."

"You can't spend the rest of your life making doughnuts."

It was a familiar argument; I could recite a hundred different versions of it by heart, with varying degrees of temper. I walked in and said cheerfully, "I got an A on my book report."

Brian, hanging onto the cupboard and trying to balance his chair absently on one leg, let it fall with a thump. "You? Got an A? In English?" he said incredulously. I opened the refrigerator and poked around. There wasn't much promising: half a jar of dill pickles, leftover meatloaf, some moldy cream cheese.

"Mom, there's nothing to eat," I complained, but she was looking at me the way Mr. Frank had looked. I should have known what was coming.

"That's wonderful. If you did it once, you can do it again. I want nothing less than A's out of you from now on."

I stared at her. Brian was grinning. "Mother," I said reasonably, "that's unreasonable—"

She got up. "So I'm an unreasonable, cranky old lady—you two have driven me there. Brian, if you don't put that chair down, you'll break your neck. You both have more brains than you're using."

"Oh, Mom," Brian groaned, and I said plaintively, "Why can't you just be glad I got an A for a change?"

"Ha," Brian said. "There's some excuse for me—I simply can't take school. But there's no excuse for you. You just can't stop with one A. That's like—that's like an artist painting just one picture, or a rock group cutting just one record—"

"Oh, quit lecturing!" I banged the empty fruit drawer shut. "You think you're so smart. The brains you have wouldn't fill the hole in a doughnut. If you're so wise about life, how come you've done nothing the past six months but sit on your—"

"Please!" My mother sighed, and lowered her voice. "Please. Don't fight in my kitchen."

"It's all right," Brian said soothingly. "She just has a hopeless crush on Neil Brown, and she's taking it out on innocent bystanders."

I had the leftover meatloaf in one hand. It would have been on his head in about two seconds, but by some miracle I restrained myself.

"You bastard."

"Joslyn!" my mother snapped, shocked. She appealed to us both. "Why can't you have some consideration for each other? Why must you always bicker? You're rational, intelligent people—why do you have to behave like two-year-olds?"

We eyed each other darkly. I took the meatloaf to the counter, and got out bread and ketchup for a sandwich. Brian lit a cigarette. He said, as our mother drew a breath, "I know, I know—not in the kitchen, not in the living room—" He paused a moment before he left; I felt his eyes on the back of my head. He said suddenly, "What are you doing?"

"What," I said coldly, "does it look like?"

"No. I mean what are you and Neil doing? It's not as if he wants to go with you or anything—"

I turned so fast I knocked the ketchup over. "Brian—"

"Brian!" said our mother. Brian shrugged a shoulder.

"Just curious," he said, and went to his bedroom. A moment later I heard his stereo. My mother put her hands on her head as if she were trying to hold it in place.

She muttered, "I'm going to move away from home."

I settled down moodily in the living room with my sandwich. Brian needed a job. He needed a padded cell or a desert island, away from people and other breakable objects. A lump of meatloaf went down cold and tasteless in my throat. Neil did care for me. He smiled when he saw me; he laughed with me; he had come to pick us up in the mountains when he hardly knew Claudia or Barbara. He just needed to wake up, as I had, to realize I wasn't the same girl he'd met barefoot with a peeling nose two years ago, just starting seventh grade. Then I realized that maybe he didn't know how I felt because I hadn't told him. Maybe all I had to do was tell him. I balanced the sandwich on my knee and thought about that. But it seemed wrong somehow; I couldn't figure out why. Erica came then, while I was thinking and switched on the TV.

It said, "Why suffer? Take Parson's Laxative, now in mint or strawberry—"

I got up and wandered out. There was no room in the world to be in love anymore.

On Wednesday, we began to paint. That was a hassle. Two old ladies stood gossiping in the yard across the street for half an hour while we parked and prayed for them to go inside. They kept giving us so many curious glances, as if they thought we were burglars, that finally we all got out of the pickup and walked down to the library. By the time we walked back, they had gone in, so we unloaded paint and brushes, thinner, newspapers, grubby clothes, and candles, and somehow got them all down the sidewalk and into the yard behind the pine trees while a police car ambled down the street. We got everything indoors finally, and changed clothes. We spread newspapers, lit candles, and contemplated the bare expanses of wall and ceiling.

I said, tired before we even started, "We need about thirty first-graders; they'd love this."

"We need a stool," Barbara said.

"We need air," Neil said. He went to one of the windows. It had been boarded on the outside, but it slid open easily. He looked at it doubtfully. It had been well boarded. But the skylight wasn't, and, straining upward he finally opened the stubborn latch. He pushed the glass as far as he could. "We shouldn't breathe paint fumes too long; it mucks up your insides."

"We won't stay that long," Barbara said. She pried open the nearest can. "Purple."

"I've got yellow," Claudia said. I reached for one.

"Black."

"Black?" Barbara said.

Neil said apologetically, "That was my bicycle, I think. I just grabbed whatever we had."

I got an inspiration suddenly, and all my tiredness left me. "That's okay. We can use it."

"We ought to get organized," Claudia murmured. She could talk in front of Neil now, once she had surprised herself into getting started. But we were in no mood to organize.

It took us a week, off and on, to do the painting, and finished, it was amazing. I painted big black and yellow sunflowers on an orange background until we ran out of yellow, and then I finished a section of wall in a patchwork of black and white squares. Claudia painted flowers with red stems and leaves since I had used all the green, too: and Barbara painted a rainbow on a black background, and copied a picture of a galaxy in gold out of an astronomy book. Neil stuck with straight painting for a while, doing the ceiling; and then he got inspired, too, and painted sea horses, goldfish, swordtails, angelfish in a gaudy orange and red sea all over the closet walls. We did all the odd leftover places in splotches of color, and the floor we painted brown—we had all kinds of brown—with big gold flowers from a can Neil had produced out of nowhere. It was beautiful. Standing in the middle of the floor, you didn't know where to look first.

By the time we were finished, we were exhausted, our hair was turning odd colors, and we had lost track of the lies we had told to explain our constant absences. I had told my parents I was doing a science project at Barbara's house, which worked fine until Barbara's mother called one day wanting to know if Barbara was at our house. So we told them Claudia was working on the project, too, and we had been at her house. But even a science project didn't explain the paint in our hair, so Barbara invented an art project, which turned out to be a mistake since everyone wanted to see it. Brian, I could tell, didn't believe any of it.

"I haven't seen Neil for days," he kept saying. "What are you up to? And why does he want my fish tank?"

Neil had bought a sea horse. He set the tank up in Barbara's house, to the joy of the twins, who gave him all their old seashells to put at the bottom of it, and crowded around him while he set up the filter.

"You can keep it here until Joe comes," he told Barbara when they were out of earshot, "then transfer it up to the house for him." His face broke into a slow smile as she watched the sea horse. It was charming, with a delicate, long-nosed face, a long curly tail, and a fat tummy that made Claudia ask hopefully, "Is he pregnant?"

"I love it," Barbara whispered, as it stared back at her from under its funny arched eyebrows, and bounced up and down in the water. "Oh, I love it. I hope it doesn't die."

Neil shook his head. "Shouldn't. It's healthy."

Mrs. Takaota, coming home then with her arms full of groceries, her face weary after a hard day with her fifth-graders, broke into a laugh when she saw it, and Barbara glanced at me triumphantly. It was a good thing to look at.

Then we began to collect things for the house on our own. That meant we didn't have to spend hours in the evenings at the house, which was a relief; we could bring whatever we found whenever we had a chance. It also meant I didn't have Neil picking me up in the evenings, or meeting me at the corner to walk to the house with me. He came over in the afternoons; he talked with me, but it seemed he would always wind up in Brian's room listening to records. It made me feel funny inside, like kicking something, but he never seemed to notice. And then one morning on Saturday he came over and asked for me. I was in my room making giant banners out of burlap and felt and colored tinfoil, which I had to do while Erica was away swimming. I had pushed all her junk under her bed and the banners lay flat on the floor. One was a landscape with felt trees and flowers and a yellow foil sun, and the other had a spaceship flying among silver stars on a blue black background. No matter how I cut the spaceship, it still looked strange, sometimes like a hot dog, and sometimes, when I tried to make it saucer shaped, like a jelly doughnut. It was giving me fits.

Then Mother called, "Joslyn! Neil wants you."

I was so surprised I almost didn't answer her. I went downstairs, licking paste off my thumb, and found him in the living room. I said, "Hello," and he said, as he had said a hundred times before in my head, "Are you busy? Can you come with me for a while?"

I nodded.

We drove to his house, which was a couple of miles away, and he took me into the garage, after introducing me to his collie, which put its paws on my stomach and licked my chin.

He said, flicking back his hair, "I got something that I wasn't sure Barbara would want. She seems to want everything to be so special. So I thought I'd ask you."

"What is it?" I asked curiously. He pointed.

"That."

"That" was a rocking chair. It was bumpy, sort of mangy, as if someone had tried to take the paint off and gotten bored. One of the arms was broken, and there was a crack in the seat. Neil put his hand on its good arm. He said, his brows crooking a little worriedly, "I know it's in bad shape. But I'm going to sand it down and refinish it. See how light the wood is under the paint? It's good, solid wood; I think it's oak. And I can fix the arm. Will she like it?"

I nodded, touching it. "Are you kidding? She'll love it. Where'd you get it?"

"Oh, some old ladies were having a garage sale down the street, and I saw it. I remembered that she wanted one. It looked so ugly I wasn't sure she'd want it in Joe's room, but I took a chance."

"How much was it?"

"Oh—" He touched the broken arm, trying to maneuver it back in place but it fell. "Not much. Really not much, considering the wood. And I have a job." He squatted down and ran his hand along the crack in the seat. "I can fill that, I think. Which would she like better on it, do you think: paint or stain?"

"I don't know." Then something struck me. "Anyway, it's for Joe. We keep talking about Barbara. What do you think he would like better?"

"Oh." He stared at the chair with a funny expression on his face. "I think just stain, so the grain will show . . ." He raised his eyes and looked at me then, and his eyes had a question in them, half-wry, half-doubtful, like the expression on his face. But something stopped the question, and he rose quickly. I felt his hand, warm and unexpected, on my arm.

"There's something else. It's in the backyard."

I would have followed him anywhere.

The other thing was a plant with green and pink leaves. It was sitting in a big coffee can; Neil said, "My mother grew about ten of these from leaves of a big plant she has; she said I could have it. I'm going to paint the coffee can. It's a coleus."

I touched a leaf. It was green on the edges, and had a smaller splotchy pink leaf shape inside. "How does it do that?" I wondered. "It's pretty. Did you tell your mother why?"

"No. I just— I said—" I looked up at him, surprised. For some reason he was blushing. He poked at the dirt under the coleus, his face lowered, and cleared his throat. "She didn't ask much. She has so many of these things. Anyway, that's what I wanted to show you. So you think they'll be all right?"

I nodded fervently. "Fine." He didn't say much after that; he drove me home in near silence. But he was okay when he let me off; he touched my arm again briefly, smiling. "Thanks, Joslyn. See you."

I went back upstairs, bemused. I felt as if I had gotten into a roller coaster that had gone over a gentle bump and stopped. I found Brian sitting cross-legged on my bed, gazing at my banners.

I said, "What do you want?"

He said, "Your spaceship is weird."

"I know." I surveyed him coldly from the doorway. "What do you want?"

He untangled himself and pointed with a bare toe. "The roof should be flatter, and you should cut a rim around the bottom."

"Huh?"

He reached for the scissors. "I'll show you." He started cutting, his tongue between his teeth. Finished, he dropped it back on the burlap: a neat, white flying saucer. I blinked.

"That's it. That's what I was trying to do—"

"Elementary. Now the question is: why?"

I looked at him. He looked at me, his chin cocked challengingly, but there was none of his usual, annoying, superciliousness in his eyes. I realized a lot, then: that he was bored, dying of curiosity, hurt because he felt left out of something Neil and I were involved in. Most of all, I remembered that Joe had been his friend.

So I said, "Joe Takaota is coming home."

He went still for a moment, his eyes holding mine, unblinking. Than he said softly, "When? What are you doing?"

I had to tell him. He said nothing when I finished; then he reached in his jeans pocket. I said, "Not in my room," and his hand came out again, even though he looked as if he hadn't heard me.

When he didn't say anything, I said nervously, "What do you think?"

He glanced at my banners, and suddenly, they looked childish to me, awkward and silly, like things you'd find in a first grade classroom. A funny lump came into my throat. Then he said soberly, "That's really a nice thing to do."

It was so unexpected I almost fell off my clogs. He cleared his throat and got off my bed. He ran his hands through his hair, and reached out to pick at a blob of paint on the window sill. He looked out the window a moment, then at me.

"Why didn't you tell me?"

"I don't know. I didn't think— I thought you'd think it was stupid or something."

"I don't think it's stupid. Why should I?"

"I don't know. You usually think everything I do is stupid."

He looked startled at that, and was silent again. Then he moved away from the window to the door. He reached out as he went by to give my hair a kind of little light pull like he used to in the years when we had been friends.

I said, "Don't tell anyone."

"Wild horses," he murmured. "Thanks. He's been in the back of my mind. I hope he's all right."

"So do I," I said softly. He didn't ask if he could help, and that was what stayed in the back of my mind for a long time.

The next evening I took my wind chimes and banners to the house, and Neil hung them from the ceiling for me. Watching him stretched between the floor and the ceiling, his face preoccupied, the copper and painted glass tinkling delicately as he hung them, I felt my mouth suddenly crowded with words. A candle gleamed in my hand; another was lit at his feet. The room was silent but for his breathing; it was so silent I could almost hear the words I wanted to say to him in the air between us before I said them.

I said, "Neil—" and stopped. The sound of my own voice scared me. He looked down at me absently, his lips parted a little, the candlelight flushing over his face. Then he winced and dropped the chime. It was the copper one so, jangling to his feet, it didn't break.

"Must've hit a beam; the tack won't go in. I threw my thumb out of joint. Let's try it over a foot."

I bent to pick up the chime. I could feel my own face burning in the light. For some strange reason I thought of Hester Prynne, then, and knew she would never have been such a coward. But I said, even before Neil could ask me what it was I had wanted to tell him, "Oh, nothing."

The next day, Monday, I hated.

It began with Barbara finding me in the morning, gripping my arm and saying as we went to our first class, "Joslyn, do you know what? I went to the pet store yesterday to get more food for the sea horse, since the twins spilled the old food all over the rug, and do you know what? Those things cost eight dollars! Neil said—he said only—I only paid him two dollars for it!"

I was startled. "Maybe he bought it somewhere else. Maybe he—" I remembered the rocking chair, then, that he had also paid a few dollars for. I said puzzledly, "Well, maybe he really wants to do something for Joe."

"Yes, but Joslyn, how will I pay him back?"

"He doesn't expect you to."

"Yes, but, Joslyn—"

I mulled it over through the bland day. Then, when we were standing in front of the school waiting for Claudia at the end of the day and talking about a Spanish test I'd just flunked, Barbara, who was still frowning, stopped mid-sentence. I saw Neil beyond her, unlocking his bike from the rack.

Barbara said, "Just a minute," and went over to him. I watched them absently. Neil straightened when Barbara came, and she talked with her hands a lot, the way she always did when she was upset, her long black hair blowing away from her face so I could see it. Neil stood listening, his hands tucked in his back pockets. He didn't say anything for awhile; he just listened, the wind picking at his hair. Then, finally, he said something. I saw Barbara's face under her dark color go scarlet.

She looked down at her feet. Then she lifted her head and looked up at him and smiled. The wind blew a strand of hair across her smile. He reached out silently, and very gently moved his hand down the curve of her cheek, down her neck, catching the strand of hair in his fingers and loosing it again to the wind.

I went home, then, alone. I went upstairs and sat cross-legged on my bed, not moving, feeling as though an ice cube were stuck, cold and hard, in my chest. I didn't think very much; I just waited for the ice cube to melt. The wind set the half-rolled blind tick-ticking against the window; an airplane droned sleepily, persistently in the sky. Somewhere outside people were talking; somebody was mowing a lawn. They were all soft, lazy sounds I had heard all my life; I never realized before how pointless they could sound. I swallowed after a while, but the ice in my chest didn't move.

Erica came in. I hardly noticed her until halfway

through doing what she called making her bed, she looked at me and asked suspiciously, "Are you sick?"

"No."

"You sound sick," she said cheerfully. "Adrian Carne stayed home from school for six days with mono. Her mother said she'd been swimming too much, but Liz Cramer says you get mono from kissing. Maybe you've been kissing too much."

That was hardly my problem. I moved a little, surprised that I could do it even with the ice cube. I said wearily, "I haven't. I wish you would shut up."

"Well don't be so polite," she grumbled. She kicked her shoes off and started looking for something, opening drawers and slamming them, picking things up and looking under them. She asked finally, "Have you seen my swim goggles?"

"No. I don't know. Look under your bed."

She went down on her knees. Her voice rose. "Well, what— Who put all this stuff under my bed? Here's my goggles, and all my overdue library books and that blouse I was looking all over for this morning. Did you— What'd you do that for?"

"I was trying to find the floor."

"Well, Joslyn—" Her voice squealed irritably, and I found myself on my feet before I even realized I moved.

"Well, God damn it," I shouted, "how am I supposed to walk in here?"

Her head came out from under the bed, flushed, surprised. I went out, down the stairs, out the front door. I walked above the flowing, oblivious evening traffic, across the park where kids squealed as they pushed each other down the slide, kept walking until I found myself in front of the deserted house. I didn't even check to make sure no one could see me. I just went in and closed the door.

The house was dark, still, musty. I took a big battery-operated lantern of Neil's we kept by the door and went to the back room. I didn't turn the light on for a while; I just sat on the floor in the dark. After a while I started to think.

I tried to figure out, from the time Neil had met Barbara on the mountain, what she had done to make him touch her face like that. She liked him, but she always seemed to be thinking more about Joe than about Neil. Girls were always chasing Neil, but she didn't even have to touch him; he had reached out for her. It didn't seem fair. She hadn't even cared until that day; she had never smiled at him like that before. She knew I liked him, and she would have been happy if he had begun finally to care for me. But he had fallen in love with her instead. It didn't make sense. I chewed on a knuckle and knew deep in me that I would have done anything—dyed my hair black, memorized my history text—to make him feel that way about me. I couldn't figure it out. I gave up finally and turned on the lantern.

Neil's fish leaped out at me: red, orange, lemon yellow; then Claudia's flowers with their strange red stems and giant faces. Barbara's galaxy looked mysterious against the black wall. My banners trailed down from the ceiling, the silver stars and yellow sun glinting in the light. The little tree in the center of the room looked strange surrounded by giant sunflowers and painted fish, and big gold blossoms on the floor. I reached out and felt the dirt under the tree, then added a little water from a can we kept for it. The wind chimes, glass and copper, hung motionless from the ceiling, above my head. The room was awkward but beautiful, half-finished, half-full of the things we had put into it, full in our minds of the things we were still going to do. I drew a deep breath, feeling better. I didn't feel cheerful; I just felt as if I might live after all, maybe.

When I got outside, I was surprised at how late it was. The sun had gone down, but it was still fairly light. I knew I would get asked where I had been, but I didn't care enough to make up a plausible lie. The stars were out by the time I got home. I could see my mother washing dinner dishes through the window. I opened the door, and the TV blared out at me, mixed with the drum of Brian's stereo.

Erica asked curiously as I came in, "Where've you been?"

"Out."

I went into the kitchen. Mother, mopping up the cupboards, arched a brow at me.

"Where have you been?"

I sat down at the table. My tongue stuck suddenly to the

roof of my mouth, so I couldn't answer. I made a face in some spilt sugar with my finger, then realized she was standing over me. Her voice changed suddenly.

"What's the matter?"

I didn't look at her because if I had looked at her I would have cried and told her, as if she could have done anything about it. I was too big to be hugged, and this hurt more than a scraped knee or a nickname, and all my pride made my tongue stick to the top of my mouth like peanut butter. So I drew a breath, realized thankfully that I wasn't going to cry, and said, "Nothing. I just don't feel too well."

My voice sounded distant and thin. She felt my face.

"You don't feel feverish. Are you hungry?"

"No."

"Did you have dinner?"

I shook my head. She opened a cupboard and I said, "I'm not hungry."

She closed the cupboard and stood silently looking down at me. Then something horrible happened. Brian came in from the backyard, and Neil was right behind him.

"Is there any ice cream?" Brian demanded.

"Don't tell me you're still hungry."

"I'm a growing boy." He opened the freezer. Neil smiled cheerfully at me, but his eyes were bright with some thought, and he wasn't really seeing me at all.

"Hi, Joslyn."

I felt as though a giant hand had got hold of me around

my middle and squeezed. I swallowed and whispered, "Hello." His brows went together; and I knew right then that if he asked me what was wrong, I would either throw the sugar bowl at him or cry. So I got out fast. I went upstairs and tried to read my science book, but it made absolutely no sense whatsoever.

I drifted fuzzily through the next day. I stared blankly for forty minutes at a history test, which demanded to know such irrelevant things as who invented the cotton gin, and what some "cross of gold" speech had been about. In science and math I stared out the window. I cut P. E. and Spanish, which Barbara and I had together; I sat in the library thinking glumly about Neil and wondering who had invented the school system anyway, and how I was supposed to be interested in amoeba and unknown numbers when someone I loved didn't love me back. I racked my brain trying to figure out what I had done wrong with Neil, what I should have done and didn't, what I had done and shouldn't have so that he didn't care for me; but I got nowhere. I was left with the bare grey fact: he liked Barbara better than me.

Well, so did I sometimes, but the thought didn't make me feel any better.

I went home by myself again that day. I went upstairs and lay down and switched on the radio. Erica came in after a while and dumped her books on her bed. With unusual tact, she didn't say anything. The phone rang, and when I didn't move, she went down to answer it.

She came back up and said, "It's for you."

"Who is it?"

"Barbara."

I didn't move for a moment. Then I rolled off the bed, sighing. After all, it wasn't Barbara's fault.

"Joslyn?" Her voice was hesitant. "Are you all right? You left so fast yesterday. I didn't see you all day today except at homeroom. Are you sick?"

"No. Yes." I couldn't make up my mind for a moment, then I decided I was. "Cramps."

"Oh." She drew a breath; her voice steadied. "Well, where were you during P. E.?"

"I cut. You know Miss Grovenor, she wouldn't excuse you from tennis if you were on the thirtieth day of your ninth month."

"Why didn't you wait for us after school? I saw you leave."

"I just—didn't feel good."

"Neil could have driven you home; he drove us home."

I almost hung up. But it was Barbara, so I drew a calm breath and said, "Oh well. I'm home. I'm just going to rest."

"Okay. Joslyn, you should see what I made for Joe's room—a giant patchwork pillow so he can sit on that if we can't find a rocking chair."

So Neil hadn't told her about his chair yet. I asked, just to be nasty, "Did he explain about the price of the sea horse?"

"Oh." She cleared her throat. "Sort of. We—he—sort of. Yes."

I let it go. "Okay. Well, I feel awful and I'm going to go collapse. I'll see you later."

"Okay. Joslyn—"

"What?"

She stuck. "I hope—I hope you feel better soon."

I went upstairs again. But I had barely gotten settled when the doorbell rang. Erica, who was downstairs, answered it. I heard footsteps on the stairs, and for one brief, desperate moment I prayed for it to be Neil. But it was Claudia.

She sat down on Erica's bed and said, "Are you sick? You didn't come home with us yesterday or today. Are you mad about something?"

I chewed on a corner of my pillow case a moment. "No. I'm not mad. I just felt like exploding, and I didn't want to do it in front of Barbara or Neil, so I thought I'd keep out of their way."

"Oh." She took it with outrageous calm. "That's a good idea. I thought it might be something serious."

"This is serious. I wish I weren't human— I wish I could walk out of my skin—"

"Well, Joslyn," she said comfortingly, "you'll find someone else."

"I don't want anyone else. No one. Ever."

A faraway look came into her eyes. "It's like Arthur and Launcelot only backwards, and you aren't married.

You aren't mad at Barbara, are you? That would be terrible."

"I'm not mad at anybody. I'm just totally—uncomfortable."

She nodded. "That's the way I feel all the time at school. But I'm used to it. I'm glad you're not angry. You're all my best friends, and I couldn't stand it if you were. How did you do on that history test today? Wasn't it easy?"

For a moment I couldn't even remember it. Then I said, "Oh. I flunked it."

She stared at me in horror. "Joslyn—"

"Well, I couldn't concentrate! How can I concentrate on McCormick reapers and carpetbaggers at a time like this?"

"Yes, but that was a midterm! You can't just flunk midterms!"

"Why not? What earthly use is knowing who invented the McCormick reaper to me? I don't even know what a reaper is."

"It's a harvest machine," she said mechanically. "It reaped— You know, harvested. As you sow, so shall you reap. You shouldn't have flunked that test, Joslyn. It's a third of your grade."

"I don't care!" I stopped because I was shouting at her. I turned over on my stomach and put the pillow over my head. I said in the dark, "I'm trying to be reasonable. I'm trying to be understanding. I'm trying not to blame anybody, or be angry, because it's no one's fault. But it takes all my effort and concentration to do it, and I simply haven't got any left over for passing history midterms."

I heard her sigh. She said in a small voice, "I'm sorry."

"You didn't do anything."

"I know, but I have to watch."

We were silent a little, then I came out from under my pillow. Surprisingly, I felt a little better. I said, "Well, I'll study hard for the final."

"I'll help you."

"Okay." I sat up, brushing at my hair. She was frowning at me anxiously, so I added, "I'm all right now. I'm human again."

"Are you sure?"

"I think so."

"Okay. I was going over to the house tonight. My mother had an old glass oil lamp in the garage that her grandmother gave her. It's pretty, especially with colored oil in it. She said I could borrow it. Is there anything you want me to take over?"

"Oh. I have some candles that have been around for ages. I'll go with you." I knew she didn't like sneaking in and out of the house alone. She cheered up.

"Okay. Shall I meet you there?"

"Can't you stay for supper?"

Her face went stiff under her smile, and I knew what she was thinking: Erica, our father, Brian and his stray friends—they would look at her, talk to her, and she would be expected to talk back with her unwieldy, hollow voice.

She said nervously, "My mother is expecting me—"

"Call her. Please stay. It felt good talking to you."

She eyed me, surprised. Her shoulders went back, and she swallowed.

"Okay."

She was fine when we went down for supper. She talked to Mom a little while I shredded lettuce for a salad. She clammed up when Erica came in, but Erica was so busy talking herself that nobody noticed. My dad came home, and Claudia looked uneasy; but he was pleased to see her since she didn't come often, and that cheered her up.

She offered to help set the table, and she was carrying some plates, her head turned to listen to something my Dad was saying, when Brian barged in, a monkey wrench in one hand, saying, "Dad, where are the battery cables? George Harmon's car—"

I don't know how he did it, but somehow the monkey wrench got tangled with the dinner plates Claudia was carrying, and they smashed in a hundred pieces all over the floor.

I've never heard that house so quiet, not even at midnight. Claudia's face was brick red; she was just on the verge of crying, and if she cried, I knew she would be too embarrassed ever to come to the house again. I wondered if she would ever forgive me for inviting her to supper. Brian looked stunned, as though he had hit her with the wrench instead of the dishes. I heard a funny snort and turned. Erica was rolled in a long-legged ball beside the table, trying to stifle her laughter in the tablecloth.

"It was—it was so funny," she whimpered. "Bri-Brian's wrench just banged into the bottom of the dishes, and they just sailed up like pancakes—and you all—you all look so funny—"

My mother drew a breath. "Erica, if you keep pulling that tablecloth, you'll have the butter in your hair."

"I'm sorry," Claudia whispered. I had a sudden, horrible thought that her voice had vanished for good.

Brian, standing helplessly in the shower of crockery, said, awed, "Oh, wow."

Claudia bent miserably and started picking up the pieces of china, and he knelt down promptly beside her to help.

My mother said dazedly, "Don't do that. Joslyn, get the broom."

"I'll sweep," Claudia whispered, but Brian's voice ran over hers.

"It's a cataclysm."

"So are you," I said crossly, giving him the broom. "Didn't your mother ever tell you not to wave a monkey wrench in the kitchen?"

"She never did." He took a sliver of china in his bare toe, then, and swore. Erica giggled. I heard a long sniff from Claudia, and my heart went cold.

"I'b sorry—" she wailed, still kneeling on the floor, and I could see the tears running down her lowered face. Brian stared at her, shocked. Then he knelt down again, fast, and put his arm around her shoulders.

"What are you crying for?" he said. "I'm the clumsy

one. I'm the one with the sliver in my toe. I'm the one with the irate mother— I'll be lucky if I get fed after this. You're just a victim of circumstances. Actually, I planned the whole thing. I had this wild, destructive impulse to just—wop those dishes with the wrench and listen to them break. Besides that, I was practicing for when I learn to play a kettledrum. Besides that—" He leaned over and whispered something in her ear. And with the tears still falling as she sniffed, she gave a little hiccup of a laugh.

I took a breath and realized that for a few moments I hadn't been breathing. I took the broom from Brian. "If you'll both get out of the middle of the kitchen floor, I'll sweep."

Our mother found her voice. "I'll feed you," she promised Brian. "Only please get that wrench out of my kitchen."

"Okay, but where are the battery cables? George Harmon's car is dead—"

"In the garage," Dad said. "Where else would they be?"

"No, they aren't," Brian said. "Sir."

"Well, where— Oh. Look in the trunk of my car. And get some shoes on!"

"Yes, sir," Brian said tolerantly. He picked his way carefully out of the broken china. I poked the broom at his feet as he left, and he pummelled me absently. My dad left the scene to us, fleeing with his drink into the living room.

My mother said, "Don't worry; they weren't especially

good. Claudia, you have shoes on; would you mind putting these bowls on the table?" She gave Claudia a stack, and Claudia, too nervous even to sniff, got them safely to the table.

She didn't talk during supper, but at least she was still there. I collected candles after we ate and put them in a grocery bag. There was a big yellow round one like a sun, and a couple of sand candles, and one shaped like a hamburger that Brian had given me for Christmas. I told my mother I was going to walk Claudia home, and she told me not to stay long. So we hurried, going across the overpass and the park, because the sun had already set. There was no one on the street when we reached the house, so we went in quickly. The moment we stepped in the door, I saw by the dim streetlight, on the living room floor that we had cleared: a crumpled bag, a newspaper, and a wine bottle three-quarters empty.

I heard Claudia stop breathing. I couldn't hear a sound in the house, but I was afraid to move. I was afraid that some drunk wanderer had heard us coming and was hiding in the dark behind a door or a corner, holding his own breath and waiting. I could feel the hair prickling up all over me, as if I were a cat. Claudia turned suddenly, reached for the door knob. It pushed back against her from outside, and we both squealed.

"Claudia—"

It was Neil. I gripped him in relief, hissing, "Neil, I think there's somebody here—"

Barbara eased in behind him, her hands full of something. Neil's head turned towards the bottle and the newspapers. He picked up the lantern beside the door and whispered, "Okay. I'll check."

"I'll come with you," Barbara whispered, but he shook his head.

"No."

"Yes."

He sighed. He turned and we all trailed behind him, following the dim, pale outline of his head while he moved soundlessly toward the kitchen. No one jumped out at him from the doorway. He moved to the bathroom, but there was no one crumpled in a corner, waiting to spring out, ragged and drunk. That left Joe's room. My stomach gave a lurch then, not in fear of whatever might be hiding in the dark, but in fear of what might have been done to the room itself. The first things Neil's light caught were my banners hanging placidly from the ceiling. They looked all right, and I started breathing again. There was no one in the closet; there was no graffiti all over the walls. The plants were still in their pots. I heard Barbara's breath loose in a sigh.

"That scared me." She was still whispering. "They could have ruined everything. I hope they don't come back. What if they come back again and next time they discover this room?"

"Maybe they won't," I said comfortingly, answering her out of habit. "They were probably just passing through."

Then I remembered she had Neil to comfort her.

She said, "I hope so. I brought the pillow. Look. Do you like it? It has a patch of everything I've ever sewn in it."

"It's neat," Claudia said. "Look. I brought an oil lamp."

"I brought candles," I said. And Neil had brought Barbara. I took the candles wearily over to one corner of the room to unpack them. Neil murmured something behind me, and Barbara, answering, made a little echo of a murmur as if their voices belonged together. Claudia came to join me.

"Where should I put the oil lamp?"

"I don't know. We really need a few tables or crates to put things on . . ." I glanced at her. Her face was back to normal again. As if she read my thoughts, she smiled a little.

"Your brother is really nice."

I said, "Brian?" as if I had ten brothers and wanted to make sure she had the right one. Then I asked curiously, since it was safe to, "What did he whisper that made you laugh, then?"

"Just something dumb. He just whispered, 'Claudia, we have to stop meeting like this.' He's really nice."

I nodded. She just liked him because he could use cataclysm in a sentence. Then I faced the fact. He had been really, unexpectedly, tactful and understanding. I wondered when he had learned how, since he never practiced in front of me. I lined the candles in a row on the windowsill, frowning. Everyone was changing around me; I didn't know any more what to expect from them. Next thing I knew, Erica would be making her bed every day, and Claudia would be waving her hand wildly to answer questions in class.

Barbara knelt next to me. She moved a candle an inch on the sill and said softly, "I'm glad you're feeling better." She didn't look at me.

I said, "I'm okay. We really need things to put things on, because we're already out of windowsills."

"Oh. Well, maybe bricks and boards . . ." She glanced back irresistably to see what Neil was doing. Three days before, I would have been the one to do that. I folded the grocery bag listlessly. Barbara rolled a candlewick back and forth aimlessly between her fingers. Her face was lowered, half-hidden behind her hair. She said helplessly, "Well. Or crates, we could paint them—"

"Who put this here?" Neil said suddenly. He was kneeling on the closet floor, looking at something. We got up.

Claudia, peering over his shoulder, said, "I didn't."

"I didn't put anything there," Barbara said. He turned his head as we came up, looking at us, a funny, wondering expression in his eyes.

"Well," he said, "whoever was here did find this room."

I had an unexpected feeling in me, then, that maybe, somehow, all the confused, half-finished, uncertain things that we were doing might make some sense after all. Whoever had wandered in from the street had come back here into Joe's room, and had stood among the painted flowers and banners. He had left on the floor beneath the painted ocean, a gift: a little collection of mussel shells, a starfish, a sand dollar, a nautilus shell—all inside a big, perfect, pink and creamy abalone shell.

Barbara and I made a sort of truce without words for a while. We had to work together, and we had to be polite; but I didn't want to talk about what had happened, and she sensed it, so we avoided the subject. Everyone at home surprised me by not being surprised at all when Neil dropped by with Barbara; the way he looked at her, touched her lightly, absently, when he spoke telling what he never said. At school, girls watched open-mouthed when Neil met Barbara at her locker in the afternoons, or walked across the street at noon with her to a hamburger stand. Neil's obliviousness made my head whirl. He treated me as he always had, like a good friend, utterly ignorant of the humiliation I was going through because of him. Brian amazed me even more. I was at his mercy; we both knew it, but he restrained himself.

So I drifted along, trying not to get hurt anymore by pushing things as far as I could to the back of my head. I was still flunking things, but that, I felt vaguely, was justifiable. I had enough to do just being civilized. Unfortunately, the education system of the State of California didn't see it that way.

I walked in the door one afternoon, thinking about some crates I had found and was going to paint for Joe's room, when my mother said, "Mr. Xanthos just called." Mr. Xanthos was my counselor, and he had been Brian's, also, unofficially, until Brian dropped out. "He said your midterm grades are so low that he's afraid you might have to repeat some of your courses if you don't shape up. He's afraid you're going the same direction as Brian went."

I dropped my books on a chair with a sigh. "I'll study hard for the finals," I promised, but she said, "No. You'll study hard now. No more running around in the evenings. I don't know what you've been doing with yourself for the past few weeks, but obviously it hasn't been studying. I want you home on school nights, and I want you to study."

"Mother—"

"I don't want another dropout under my feet all day."

"I'm not going to drop out! I just can't— I just can't concentrate. Nothing they're teaching me seems very important. They're teaching me all the wrong things."

She was silent a moment, looking at me. Her voice softened a little. "Well, some things you have to be taught, and other things nobody in the world knows how to teach you."

I sat down on the couch beside her and propped my feet on the coffee table. I wished a funny thing then: that I was small enough again to curl up in her lap, even though I was as tall as she was, and even though she didn't have too many answers.

I said, "Oh, I know. But please don't ground me during the week."

"Joslyn—"

"Mom, I'll study! I swear it! But I'm doing—what we're doing—I just have something special to do, and it's very important, really important, and I have to be able to work on that, too. I'll come home from school and study, I promise, but sometimes I'll have to go out—I have to."

"What are you doing?"

"It's something with Barbara and Neil and Claudia—you know them—they wouldn't do anything that wasn't right. Especially Neil. You know that. I'll study—"

She sighed. "I've heard that before."

"The last time I promised to study, I did. Remember? And I got an A. I can do it again. I'll do it again."

She was silent again, frowning at me. She reached out absently and brushed the hair away from my face so she could see it. "What are you four doing?"

I drew a breath. I wanted to tell her, but I knew it would be better to present her with the accomplished fact, rather than have her all upset about trespassing and illegal entry and other things. "It's not quite finished yet. It's a very special surprise for someone. It's something really important. When it's done, I'd like you to see it. But not now. Can you trust me?"

She smiled a little, wryly. "I can trust you to worry me grey-haired. All right. But I want to see you every afternoon studying. I'll tell Erica to keep her friends downstairs while you're working. I want you to start now."

"Now?"

"Now. What have you got for homework?"

I sighed. "Oh, there's a test in English tomorrow on *The Merchant of Venice*—"

"Have you read it?"

"Ah—not all of it. And there's a quiz in Spanish, but it's just a little vocabulary test, not like a midterm or anything, and there's a chapter in history and some science questions. That's it, I think. Oh, and a page of algebra."

"All right. If you finish all that at a reasonable hour, you can go out. But I want to see all your tests from now on. In fact . . ." She paused and let that thought go. I stood up and gathered my books.

"All right. But I can't do all this on an empty stomach."

I collected some cookies, a glass of milk and a dill pickle and took them upstairs with me. The room was a mess. I couldn't even find my desk, and I decided, surveying it as

I ate the pickle, that I couldn't possibly study in that environment. So I made my bed and Erica's, and started unburying the desk. There were books, papers, stuffed animals, pieces for a dress I had cut out but hadn't made, a scrapbook, a swim fin, campaign buttons, balloons, and colored pencils all over it. I wandered around trying to find places for everything, but all the drawers and the closet shelves were full. When I got to the scrapbook, I opened it because I hadn't seen it for ages. There on the front page was me in a long flowery dress with Juliet sleeves, standing beside Gilbert Hill. I chewed on a cookie, looking at him. He did look skinny, sort of shrimpy. And I looked strange with my hair all curly. I sat down on the bed and turned a page. There was a ribbon I had won at a relay race on Field Day that year, and a pink garter I had made for a part in some class play when I was a barmaid in a saloon. I turned another page. Then I realized someone was standing in the doorway watching me.

It was Brian. He had a funny look on his face. He waited while I rechannelled a cookie crumb I had sent down my throat the wrong way out of surprise, then he said briskly, "I'm supposed to help you study."

I yelped, "What?"

He sat down on the bed and looked through my books. "It's a paying proposition: two bucks an hour, and a bonus if you get A's. What have you got to do?"

I stared at him, dumbfounded. Then I raised my voice. "Mother!"

"Oh, *The Merchant of Venice*. I had that, too. Have you read it?"

"Mother!"

"Have you read it?"

"I can't understand all those weird words. Moth—"

"Quit yelling; she went to the supermarket. What weird words?"

I said irritably, "We have to memorize some speech that doesn't make any sense. 'The quality of mercy is not strained—' We have to be able to write it line for line, and I don't even know what it means. I know mercy isn't strained, it's not orange juice. It doesn't make sense."

He mulled it over, picking at his thumbnail with his teeth. "Oh. It's not strained like orange juice; it's more like muscle strain—"

"What?"

"You know, when you're straining—trying really hard to do something. Being merciful isn't something you should strain to do—it's something that comes naturally, droppething like the gentle rain from heaven—"

"Brian—"

His voice sharpened. "Shut up and listen. I need a new guitar, and you're going to get A's if it kills you."

I nearly killed him that first afternoon. He took me page by page for three hours through *The Merchant of Venice;* he breathed down my neck while I did algebra, pouncing on me when I made mistakes; he hammered Spanish vocabulary and history dates and science terms at me until I was ready to throw things at him. At one point we were both shouting: he asking history questions at the top of his voice, and me yelling dates back at him because I was furious with him, and tired and hungry. And then I heard myself shout 1865, the year the Civil War ended, and it struck me as such a funny thing to be shouting that I just started laughing. Brian caught it, too; he collapsed on Erica's bed and put the open book over his face. We laughed until we hurt.

At nine we both came down. I could smell food from the kitchen, and my insides ran together for a moment. Mom and Dad were sitting at the kitchen table having a peaceful cup of spiked coffee. They smiled at us as we came in.

"How did it go?" Dad said.

"Ask her anything," Brian said. There was a note of deep pride in his voice. "Ask her the Quality of Mercy speech, backwards or forwards. Ask her how many years it takes the sun to go around the center of the galaxy once. Ask her to say, 'I like meatballs,' in Spanish. Go ahead, tell them."

"*Me gustan las albóndigas,*" I said obediently. "Also, las fried chicken and what kind of pie is that?"

"Cherry," my mother said. I staggered over to it.

*"Soy muerto de hunger."*

"Me, too." Brian sighed, sinking into a chair. He roused himself to open one reddened eye and glare at me. "Tomorrow you get an A on that English test."

I swallowed a mouthful of cherry pie. "I have to go through this every afternoon?" I said incredulously. "He's a slave driver; all he cares about is money. I'll die of knowledge just so he can make money off my brains."

My mother choked on her coffee. "Don't worry. That's one thing nobody ever died of."

I made an A on the English test. I knew that even before I finished it, because I went through it amazed that it was so easy. I was dumbfounded. So was Claudia, when I told her after school, putting books in our lockers.

"How'd you do that?" she demanded.

"Brian helped me. It was either that or be grounded," I admitted, and she grinned.

"That's so good."

"And I only missed two in my Spanish quiz—got my sexes wrong. And in history usually I don't pay any attention because it's so dull, and I don't have the vaguest idea of what's going on, but today I kept hearing things I knew something about, and my ears just kept listening. It was like getting a hearing aid."

"What was?" said Barbara behind me and I turned to answer. Then I looked at her, and I couldn't answer. Her face went bright with color, so I made my tongue move.

"Brian—Brian's been helping me study."

"Oh." She added after a second, "That's good." There was something else in her face I couldn't read.

There was a little silence; then I said to Claudia because I knew Barbara would go home with Neil, "You coming home now?"

Her eyes went to Barbara's face. Then they dropped. "No."

"What are you going to—" I stopped. There was a funny look on her face, too, and suddenly I didn't think I wanted to know what she was going to do. Barbara drew a breath.

"Joslyn, we're going to the fabric shop for some pillow stuffing. And—and also I decided to make some curtains for Joe's room, because the windows are so ugly."

"Oh." I was more surprised than anything else that they hadn't asked me to come with them. But she wasn't finished. Her eyes lifted then, holding mine. Her voice was very soft.

"Also, I have to buy some material for a Junior Prom dress."

I stared at her, stunned. The Junior Prom was something vague, distant, that belonged in the future, like learning to drive, or getting wisdom teeth. "You're going to— But who—" I stopped dead. She swallowed.

"That day when I was upset about the price of the sea horse, he asked me. Just out of the blue. He— I told him he should ask someone from his own class, but he said— he said—"

"Oh," I whispered.

"I didn't think you would want to come with me today, so I didn't—" Her voice shook and she stopped. I remembered then that I had arms and legs, and they could move. I took a step back.

"Oh. Well. I have to— I have to go home anyway and study, I'm supposed to. So—" I took another step back and bumped into someone. I saw Claudia close her eyes.

"Hi, Joslyn," Neil said, steadying me with one hand. "What are you all looking so somber about?"

All the blood in me rushed into my face. I wanted to shrivel into a leaf and blow away. I didn't know what to say. I wanted to be polite, but my tongue felt too big for my mouth and it wouldn't move. So I gave up helplessly and just walked away down the hall, and my back felt as if a thousand eyes were crawling all over it. My feet walked home without the rest of me knowing what they were doing. I tossed my books on the couch, and went upstairs, wanting to crawl under all my bedcovers and stay in the dark for awhile. But I couldn't. Brian was lying on my bed, waiting.

I found my voice when it moaned. "Oh, no, please, not now—"

"Let's see your English test. Where are your books?"

"Brian, I can't—I can't—"

He fixed me with an evil eye. "Go get your books."

"Brian, please—"

"What'd you get on your English test?"

"I flunked it," I said desperately.

"You did what?" Then he settled back composedly. "You got an A. Didn't you? Didn't you?"

I snarled at him and went down to get my books. Erica, eating ice cream with her friends in the living room, grinned at me mockingly. I snarled at her and dragged myself back upstairs.

We finished at a more reasonable hour that day. I had supper, then went to the backyard to paint some crates I had found for Joe's room. I painted one crate leaf green and the other lemon yellow, colors my mother had left over from when she painted the kitchen. They looked nice when they were done, and I felt a little calmer. It was quiet in the back; the sun had set but the sky was still blue grey with dusk. I sat back on my heels and sniffed. I could smell cool grass, a faint smell of cypress from our yard. The night smells made me restless; I wanted to go somewhere, do something. I thought about calling Claudia, but something inside me winced away from that idea. So I just lay on the swing for a while, thinking about nothing and watching the stars come out. Barbara's voice coming unexpectedly out of the darkness made me jump.

"Joslyn?"

I sat up. She had come around the side of the house; I hadn't heard the gate. I said, "Watch out for the paint."

"Oh." She dodged the cans and came over to me. She didn't sit down. I couldn't see her face very well; it was silhouetted against the bright light from Brian's room. She said haltingly, "Neil—Neil and I came by to see if there is anything you want taken to the house. He's got the truck. I made— I finished the curtains."

"That was fast."

"Well, they were easy—just a seam and a hem. I got some gold cotton lining; it was really cheap, and I thought it would match the floor." She paused. I tried to think of something to say, but my brain felt empty. She went on quickly, "I was able to do it this afternoon because my mother was out; otherwise she would have seen them."

"Oh."

There was another little silence. She drew a breath, moving a little toward me, and said pleadingly, "Joslyn—"

But I didn't want to talk about it. I said quickly, "Are you and Neil going out?"

"Yes, to a movie."

"On a school night?"

"Well, my mother said with all the babysitting I do, I need a night out away from the twins. Joslyn—"

"I wish my parents would give me a night away from studying."

"Joslyn, I have to tell you. Joe's coming home Saturday."

I felt a funny prickling down my back. Sometimes, working on the room for him, I forgot who it was for; I forgot he even existed, and that he was coming to look at it out of his dark, hurt eyes. I swallowed. "I hope he likes it."

"Oh, Joslyn, so do I," she whispered. "Do you know what? I'm scared." She broke off as a window slid up behind her. Neil, in Brian's room, stuck his head out.

"Barbara? We'd better go. Joslyn, we're taking the rocking chair over tonight; it really turned out well. Is there anything we can take for you?"

"No, thanks," I said.

Barbara said reluctantly, "Well. Well, I'll see you later."

"Yeah."

She left. A moment later I saw her in Brian's room, her face lifted, smiling at something Brian said. Then Brian went out, and they turned to follow him. Neil's hand slid up Barbara's back to cup gently the curve of her head beneath her hair. His face turned toward her; in the bright light I saw his clean profile, the trimmed, pale hair, and the little, sweet smile he gave her. Then they went out, and he reached back to shut off the light. And sitting in the swing, hugging my knees, I cried, finally, like a little kid crying for something it couldn't have.

I felt better afterward, sort of damp and clean inside. I waited for a while for the red to go out of my eyes and nose. Then I went in the house. It was quiet. Brian had gone somewhere, and my parents were in bed. Upstairs, Erica was reading. She glanced at me when I came in, and I knew from the way her eyes went right back to her book that I looked as if I had been crying.

She didn't say anything while I got undressed. Then, as I threw back the covers and plopped down on the bed, she said tentatively, "You know what I was thinking?"

"What?"

"I was thinking we ought to rearrange the bedroom."

I gave a short laugh. "We could, if we can find it."

"I know it's messy. But I was thinking if we moved the beds apart and put your things on one side of the room, and mine on the other, then I could have my side messy

and you could keep yours clean. What do you think?"

I thought about it. "It might work. We could move the beds one on each side of the window."

"And a dresser at the foot of each bed."

"And the desks on each side of the closet."

She nodded eagerly. "And you could have the top shelf of the closet, and me the bottom. Or—" she added hastily, "me the top and you the bottom; I don't care."

"Or we could divide the closet right down the middle, too, since that's where the dividing line is anyway."

"Yeah. Don't you think that's a good idea?"

"Sure." I rolled over, pushed my pillow under my stomach, and rested my head on my hands. "What about the bedside table and the lamp? We both use them."

"You can have them; you use them more than I do."

"You're using the lamp now."

"Well, there must be another one around somewhere. I'll look."

"Okay." She was quiet a moment. She reached up and switched off the light. Then in the darkness, she said, "You know what? Promise you won't tell anyone. Promise?"

"I promise," I said tolerantly.

"There's this boy on the swim team I really, really like . . . He's got brown hair and green eyes. His name is Jerome."

"Jerome?"

"Yeah. Isn't that a neat name? Do you know what? I

think I'll grow my hair long. How long did it take you to grow yours long?"

I thought back sleepily. "I was in seventh grade when I got it cut last."

"Two years . . . He just moved here from Oregon. He's in my classes. Once when we were horsing around before practice, he dunked me. But I think he likes Cher Adams better than me. That's why I want to grow my hair long. He likes long hair."

I grunted. "Good luck."

"I can't help it. I just like him." That made me smile; I didn't know why. She was silent again. Then she said, "Joslyn?"

"Mm."

"What are you and Neil and Claudia and Barbara doing?"

I rolled over and stared at the darkness. We hadn't just talked like this in a long time, and suddenly, for some reason, I couldn't put her off with a lie or tell her to mind her own business. She was nearly as tall as I was, and she had fallen for a kid named Jerome who dunked her, and she knew about Neil and Barbara, but instead of teasing me about it, she was trying to be nice to me. So I said, "We're trying to do something for Joe Takaota."

"Joe—what happened to him? Nobody ever told me."

I told her.

She said, awed, when I finished, "How terrible. That must've hurt. I wouldn't do that for a million dollars. I'd take sleeping pills first—"

"Erica! Don't even say that! Don't even think it!"

"All right," she said, surprised. "But why did he do it?"

"I don't know. Just because things got rough, I guess, in his head. He couldn't stand thinking about them any longer."

"What are you doing for him?"

I thought of the little room in the middle of a small, tired, empty house, in the middle of a great mass of towns and cities. I wondered then if the things in it that we had found so beautiful: the plants and banners, pillows and wind chimes and paintings, were really what the part of him still trying to stay alive was looking for. I knew then what Barbara had meant when she said she was scared. She was afraid of Joe, afraid the person she was expecting wouldn't be the same person who would walk into that room on Saturday. I swallowed. The back of my mouth was dry.

"I don't know."

Claudia was waiting for me beside my locker the next morning. I saw her from a distance, but I kept coming because I had to face her some time, and she would have been hurt worse than I was if I'd turned away. Her face was colorless except for her nose.

I said, "Hi," and she said miserably, "Joslyn, I'm sorry about yesterday. I felt awful. So did Barbara. But you—but there's just nothing—"

"I know." I dropped my books on the floor and whirled the dial on the lock. "Did she find some nice material?"

"Yes. White with little burgundy-colored flowers all over it. You're still mad."

"I'm not mad." And suddenly, when I said that, it was true. I sat down on the pile of books on the floor and said tiredly, "I'm not mad. There's nothing—there's nothing to be angry about. It's just—I'm just—" I didn't know what I was just. "I'm going to go be a hermit."

"You could be a nun," she whispered, "like Guinevere."

"A nun." The bell rang and I got off my books.

She didn't move; she looked at me anxiously so I said, "It will be all right."

I meant it, so she believed me.

I didn't talk to Barbara for a few days. I wasn't angry; I just didn't feel like talking. I wanted to avoid Neil, too, but I would rather have died than have him guess the way I had felt about him, so I tried to treat him normally, like a friend. But, hanging the crates for me in Joe's room one evening, he glanced at me and said softly, "You're so quiet."

I didn't know what to say. I shrugged a shoulder, which was a little hard to do while holding a crate steady on a wall. "I'm just tired. Studying too hard, I guess."

He went back to his pounding. He had to pound gently, and it was slow work. He had put one beside the closet, and he was hanging the other near Barbara's galaxy. She had put the rocking chair beneath it, and a small brick and board shelf full of science fiction paperbacks beside it. When Neil hung the crate, I was going to put Claudia's oil lamp in it so Joe would have reading light. On the other side of the room, Barbara had put the pillows she made, plump and bright, with another little shelf between them holding candles, plants, a wooden flute.

Looking around at the room, I said surprisedly, "It is beautiful."

Neil gave a nail a final tap and smiled. "I didn't know it would turn out so well. I really didn't."

"What will— What will Joe think of it? He's not—I mean, I never knew him. I never really knew who we were making this place for. And now that he's coming, I don't know if it's right for him. Even Barbara. I don't think even she knows."

He centered the last nail and give it a meditative whack. He said simply, "I don't know what Joe will think. I was doing it for Barbara."

"Then you don't know if it's right, either."

"No. We can hope it is."

"You knew Joe—"

He shook his head. "Nobody did."

I was silent again. I had thought in the beginning that we all knew what we were doing, but now it seemed none of us knew. Neil finished driving the nail in and gave the crate a tug to see if it would hold. I was getting over being in love with him, but it was slow work, and some place in me still felt sad when I was with him. He said, "Okay," and I put the oil lamp in it, centering it. We stood back to look at it.

"It looks nice," I said glumly. He glanced at me. Unexpectedly, he put a hand on my shoulder, shaking me a little.

"Don't be so worried. The important thing is that he has people to do something like this for him. He's lucky."

I wanted to shout at him that I wasn't sad about Joe but about me, and it was all his fault even if he was too stupid to realize it. Then, looking at him, for a split second I wondered if he really did know everything that had happened and was simply trying to handle it, as we all were, as best he could. I looked away from him. His hand tightened a little, then dropped, and he stretched to get the kinks from hammering out of him. He picked up the left-over nails and the lantern.

He said suddenly as we went out, "And Barbara's lucky, too, that she has you to help her do this."

I didn't answer. But part of my brain kept chewing on what he had said even after he drove me home, even after I went to bed.

The next afternoon, Claudia had a doctor's appointment to discuss her operation, so she didn't meet me to walk home together. I got my books absently, trying to see her in my mind's eye, wondering if she would come out ravishingly beautiful. I decided probably not, with her pale eyebrows and round, pink face, but she would look better, and that would make her happy. Slamming my locker shut and turning, I came face to face with Barbara. She said softly, "Will you walk home with me?"

I nodded. I found my voice, as we walked outside. "Where's Neil?"

"He's at a Student Council meeting. Joslyn, he got some fish to go with the sea horse. They're orange and pink, like candy." She was silent a little. It was a hot Friday afternoon, so hot I could smell the leaves baking in the sun. I could feel the sun burning my nose under my tan. Barbara said, "Joslyn—" and stopped. I knew what she wanted to say; I didn't know yet what I would say when she did.

I said, "We'll have to move the fish tank to the house tonight, then."

She nodded. "And make sure everything's ready. I don't— I'm not sure how I'll tell him about it. But I'll think of something."

I considered that blankly. "That might be hard. That might be harder than anything any of us have done."

"It's all right; I'll think of something." I heard her take a breath to say something, but she didn't. I heard the sound again, a moment later. Then she stopped in the middle of the sidewalk, facing me, so that I had to stop, too. She said, "Joslyn, I miss you."

I looked back at her silently. I didn't know what I wanted to answer. Then one of my shoulders spoke before I could, giving a little shrug, saying, Oh well. Her face was puckered in little worried lines; it was as familiar to me as my own face. It made me smile suddenly, because I knew it so well. I said, "Oh well."

"I'm sorry—"

"It's all right."

"You sure?"

"Yeah."

She gave a deep, relieved sigh. We fell into step again.

"I'm so glad. There are so many things I want to tell you, but I couldn't; and who else can I tell them to, if not you and Claudia? I felt awful, when I couldn't talk to you."

"Well, I couldn't talk to you either—the only person I had to talk to was Brian, and all he ever says is 'Did you make an A on your algebra test?' "

"Did you?"

"Of course not, but at least I'm not flunking any more. What pattern did you get for your prom dress?"

"It's really simple, just floor-length, sleeveless, with a-a sort of plunging neckline. Joslyn, I couldn't believe it when he asked me. He just— One moment he was just somebody I didn't know very well, who was really nice, and the next minute he just—the next minute I loved him. He just looked at me—"

I nodded. If Claudia had been there, she would have said something about Romeo and Juliet. Barbara was trying to gesture excitedly with her arms full of books; her face was really happy. Everything she had had to hold back came spilling out of her then; and in the hot, lazy afternoon, I felt too peaceful to be jealous. When we reached her house, Mrs. Takaota said, "Joslyn, I haven't seen you for ages!" and the twins dragged me to the fish tank to see the new fish, which flashed in the salty water, gaudy as Lifesavers.

I had supper with Barbara. Neil dropped by in the middle, and Mrs. Tataota fixed a plate for him, too, in spite of all his protests. He grinned at me.

"You're supposed to be home studying."

I put my hands over my mouth. "Oh, I forgot. How did you know?"

"Brian told me. He came into the doughnut shop one night and said he had a job and you were going to make straight A's this semester."

I made a face. "Not after the way I got started. I really forgot. I'd better go home."

"It's Friday," Mrs. Takaota said. "Finish your dinner."

"I can't. I promised my mother I'd study if she promised she wouldn't ground me. Brian's probably been waiting for me. All he cares about is money."

Neil shook his head. "He misses going to school."

"He what?"

"But he's afraid to come back, afraid of being behind everyone else in his class. He's got a lot of brains. He really likes teaching you."

I eyed him incredulously. Mrs. Takaota said, "Finish your dinner," and Neil said, "I'll drop you off at your house. Finish your dinner."

So I did. I got home to find my mother washing dishes. She looked at me coldly. I sighed and said pleadingly, "I forgot! I was at Barbara's and I didn't remember until right in the middle of dinner. Besides, it's Friday—"

She dropped a plate into the dish drainer. "It's a school day. You are supposed to come straight home and study."

"I know. I know. I just forgot. Besides, if I study on a Friday, how am I supposed to remember everything until Monday? Besides, I don't have much homework."

"That's not the point. You need to learn to discipline yourself. We made a bargain: you were to go out only after your homework was done. You didn't keep your part."

I drew a breath. I was on shaky ground. "I have been. I've been working hard, you know that. I just forgot once —just once. I'm not perfect. I can't be disciplined overnight. I am trying; I have been doing a lot better."

"So far, yes. But if you can't remember to come home to study, how will you learn anything? You've been scatterbrained all year; you need something to help you remember—"

"Mother—" I said desperately, before she committed herself to saying anything rash.

"I'm not going to go through another of my children dropping out of school."

"Mom, you promised you wouldn't ground me!"

"And you promised something to me, too. From now on—"

Whatever it was she was going to say, Brian interrupted with a sudden, melodramatic, "Halt!" We both turned. He was standing half-naked in the doorway, sweaty and greasy from working on a car. Having caught our attention, he went on more gently to my mother, " 'The quality of mercy is not strained. It droppeth as the gentle rain from heaven upon the place beneath. It is twice blessed: it blesseth him that gives and him that takes . . .' "

He ran through it to the end, stopping only once for a cue. I was fascinated. So was our mother. She listened with-

out moving, letting the hot water run behind her. When he finished, he gave us a little bow and said, "Defense rests. Is there any beer in the house?"

My mother gave him a glass of cold water dazedly.

I said, "How many years does it take the sun to go once around the center of the galaxy?"

He gulped water. "Two hundred-million years."

"How do you say, 'I am tired,' in Spanish?"

*"Soy cansada."*

"Who invented the McCormick reaper?"

He wiggled a brow at me. "P. J. Sullivan."

My mother cleared her throat. "When are you going back to school?"

He shrugged. "First I have to get George Harmon's car fixed." He pointed a finger at me. "You. I'll see you in the driveway in five minutes. Bring your books."

So I did homework for an hour, sort of, reading aloud to Brian's feet as they stuck out from under the car.

We finished Joe's room that night. Neil picked Claudia and me up in the truck; Barbara rode behind, keeping the fish tank steady in the back. We waited a few blocks away until it grew really dark, then Neil parked around the corner from the house, and one by one, carrying things, we slipped in. We got the fish and the sea horse settled in the tank again; we watered plants and dusted candles and picked the fuzzballs out of corners. Claudia added shells from her own collection here and there: a conch, a sand dollar, tiny butterfly shells with delicate wings. When there wasn't anything more to do, we still wandered aimlessly around straightening candlewicks, moving things over an inch, then back again.

Finally Barbara said, "We'd better go."

We left one at a time, since it was Friday night and the cops would be out full force. I got home about ten-thirty; no one was there but Erica, watching television. I plopped down in a chair and took my shoes off, tired for some reason. I wanted to tell someone what we had done, and that it was all finished and beautiful, but there was no one to tell. So I watched TV until I dozed off on the couch.

I didn't see Barbara at all the next day. I didn't expect to, but still I was restless with curiosity and anticipation, wondering if Joe were well, if the house was right for him. Neil stopped by on his bike in the afternoon to add his head to the circle of heads around George Harmon's car. I knelt on the back of the couch and watched moodily. Every time they turned the engine on, the oil dipstick would shoot straight up into the air, and the crowd of bent bodies would scatter hastily, laughing and swearing. It was the most exciting thing that happened all day.

Neil saw me eventually and came in for a moment. He said, "Have you heard from Barbara?"

"No. Have you?"

"No."

"What's the matter with the car?"

He wiped sweat off his face with his arm and said wonderingly, "I've never seen anything like it."

And that was that.

The next day, Claudia came by. I was lying on the swing

in the backyard, trying to get a tan on my back and reading a book with half my mind. I moved over for her and she sat down. She raised her knees and propped her chin on them. Obviously she had something on her mind, so I waited.

"I'm having the operation next Saturday."

I rocked the swing gently with one foot. "You scared?"

She nodded. "I hate the part where they give you a shot to put you to sleep, and I get sleepier and sleepier but I make myself wake up because I don't like that kind of sleep. I hate hospitals. I hate having to be like this. I don't see why I was born this way instead of someone else."

"I don't know why either." She rarely complained about it, but the operation was depressing her. I said comfortingly, "You'll come out with a new face, though. You'll be prettier."

"I'll just be more normal. My face isn't pretty. It's all round and my eyes are round and my hair is fuzzy."

"Well, faces change. It'll grow up one of these days."

"I think I wouldn't mind, if my hair were just straight and thick and long."

"Grow it. It's a pretty color."

"It's too frizzy to grow straight."

"Iron it."

She looked at me. Then she smiled a little. "I wouldn't dare. I'd burn it up. I wouldn't dare . . ." She gave a little sigh then and came out of it. "Have you heard from Barbara?"

"No."

"I wonder if everything's all right."

The side gate banged then, and Brian came into the yard. He didn't see us for a moment; he just stood with his head bowed, his hands jammed into his back pockets. Then one hand groped around in the pocket and he pulled out his cigarettes. He looked strange for some reason. I realized why finally. He had a shirt on, and it was tucked in.

I called to him, "Been to church?"

His head turned, and he looked as if he didn't know whether to answer or not. Then his feet brought him over to us and he sat down next to Claudia. He put his arm around her, and she blushed.

"Hi, honey."

She was too embarrassed to answer, but she was grinning. He let her go and shook his cigarette pack. It was empty; he looked at it blankly. Then he leaned back, tilting his face to get the sunlight and said, "I just went over to see Joe."

I sat up. "How is he?"

He shrugged a shoulder, his eyes hidden. "All right, I guess. I guess. He said he wanted to go back to school, said I might as well keep him company. He hasn't changed much . . ."

"Is that good or bad?"

"I don't know." He was silent, then he made a restless, wiggling movement. He said almost angrily, "How do I know? How should I know? He was smiling with the twins sitting on his lap. But how do I know what he's got locked in his head from the past few months?"

"He could tell you," Claudia said. "You're his friend."

I stared at her. I had never heard her voice so clear and steady when she was talking to someone besides Barbara or me. And Brian didn't even notice; he just answered her as if a miracle hadn't just happened under his nose, "I was his friend before. He didn't tell me then what was in his head. I didn't do him any good then."

"Well, maybe he'll use you this time."

He looked at her. "That's a funny way to put it."

She flushed under his eyes, her voice going unsteady again. "Well, that's what friends are for, sometimes. You use them to help you. You have to. Who else will help?"

He looked down, using both hands to ruffle his long hair wildly, like a dog. "I suppose so." He didn't sound angry anymore. He turned to her again and said soberly, "I'll be there. I don't know— I don't know if that will do any good because I don't know where he's at, and I'm afraid for him. But I'll be there." He got up to go. Then he said, "Oh. Barbara said tonight at nine. She said to tell you, and you'd know what it meant."

"Do you want to come?"

He shook his head. Then he ruffled his hair again and nodded. "I'll come."

I rode to Claudia's house about seven because I was afraid my mother would invent some reason at the last minute to keep me home. Claudia and I played gin nervously for an hour and a half; then we put the cards away and just walked out of the house without talking, without telling anyone where we were going. It was fairly dark; the stars were surfacing in a blue grey sky. It wasn't cold, but I felt cold; I walked with my hands under my arms. We didn't say much as we walked to the house. By the time we reached it, the sky had darkened; the pines in front of the house were shapeless with shadow. The street was quiet. We slipped in and found Neil in Joe's room, lighting candles.

He smiled at us, his face drenched in matchlight. Candles burned like stars in the crates, on the floor in front of the curtains and bookshelves, in the closet. Their hot, shifting air stirred the chimes: every few seconds they would give a little tinkling sigh of glass or copper. The sea horse was watching us, his nose pressed against the glass, his tail curled like a question mark, while the pink and orange fish wound through the plants like birthday ribbon. A candle on the shelf of books lit up the galaxy, all Barbara's careful dots of gold whirling together towards a gold orange core. Another one on the closet floor shook its shadow across the sea, so all Neil's fish seemed to be rippling, moving. The little tree, the coleus, the fuschia Neil had brought, the daisies I had borrowed from my mother's garden, the little nameless plants we had bought for forty-nine cents at the supermarket trailed down the crates, curled over the books, made little splashes of green in dark corners, in unexpected places. The banners moved gently above our heads, shaking their silver stars and flowers. I leaned against the doorway, feeling as though I were in some strange church, or in a spaceship, or somewhere just beyond the edge of the world. I didn't even hear anyone come in until Barbara touched me.

I turned. Joe's dark eyes were looking beyond me for a second, but he brought them back to me while he said, "Hello, Joslyn," softly. He looked a little heavier than when I had last seen him, and his face seemed shapeless, blurred, but that could have been the candlelight. There was no expression on it. Brian was behind him. Joe went past me slowly, moving into the room. Brian stood beside me, watching.

Joe stopped in the middle of the room, taking it in with a quick glance. In the flickering light, I saw his face still expressionless, but his eyes moving. His hand went out to the tree first, stopping a second in front of it as if it were a flame and he were warming himself. Then he touched its webbed branches gently. He touched a butterfly shell and ran his fingers down the flute. He stopped in front of the galaxy Barbara had painted, and studied it until he saw the sea horse out of the corner of his eye. His head jerked toward it; he went to the tank, squatted in front of it. He turned his head to look at us briefly, wordlessly. He touched the coleus with its pink and green leaves above the tank, and then he saw the books Barbara had brought for him. He went toward them, but he didn't reach them. He stopped, his head thrown back, to look at my banners.

Then he turned and stopped again, facing one of the long, thin gold curtains Barbara had made. A wind chime tinkled a few notes softly above it. He didn't move. All I could see was the back of his head.

His hand moved out slowly, flicked the two lengths of curtain apart. He felt for the window catch and slid the window up easily, almost absently. He reached out. His hand stopped flat on the solid board beneath it.

My parents were waiting up for me when I got home. It was late, almost midnight on a Sunday night, and they didn't look very happy with me. My father, who had to get up at six the next morning, looked at me a little bleary-eyed and demanded, "Joslyn, where have you been?"

I glanced at the clock. "I'm sorry," I said weakly. "I didn't realize it was so late." I didn't want to argue; I wanted to curl up in a ball on the couch, but they were both sitting on it. I added helpfully, "You can go ahead and ground me; it's all right now."

That stopped them a moment. My mother said, "Where have you been?"

"In the park."

"With whom?"

"Claudia and Barbara."

"At this time of night? What were you doing?"

I shrugged a shoulder. "Nothing. Just sitting, mostly. Just—sitting."

"Was Brian with you?"

"No," I said, surprised. "He's not home? I don't know where he went after—"

"After what?"

I sighed. "After— After—" Everything was stuck in the back of my throat. After Joe had said politely, perfunctorily, the kinds of things you say when someone gives you a shirt or a pair of shoes you wouldn't be caught dead in; after we had walked him home in the most embarrassing silence I had ever been a part of in my life. I wondered vaguely if Brian would ever speak to me again for submitting him to that. I wished there was a way of walking out of my body.

"After—" I was stuck again. Then I saw the way my mother was looking at me, her anger turning to bewilderment, concern; and a lump of self-pity rose in my throat.

"Joslyn," she said, alarmed, and I sat down in a chair next to them.

My dad said brusquely, "What happened?"

So I told them. I told them about the house we had broken into and the tree we had stolen. I told them about all our lying, and all our cautious sneaking around after dark, in and out of the house, as we brought in paint, candles, books, crates, flowers. I told them about the sea horse Neil bought, about Neil and Barbara, about Neil and Barbara and me. I told them everything. When I finished finally, the house sounded dead still without my voice. The clock's hands had jumped forward almost an hour.

My dad cleared his throat. "The important thing is that you tried."

I shook my head wearily. "I don't think that's true. Because if it is, how come we all feel so rotten? Nobody wants to talk about it. Brian wouldn't even talk to me, and he didn't even have anything to do with it. I wish we had never— I wish we had never thought of it in the first place."

My mother rubbed her eyes with her fingers. "I knew you must be doing something like that—something that complicated, but I never— I never imagined anything like this. It sounds beautiful."

"It just sounds that way." But when I said that, I knew it wasn't true. I loved what we had done to that room more than anything I'd ever done in my life. It was the most beautiful place in my mind.

"I'd like to see it," my dad said.

"We'll, I'll tell you where it is. But I won't take you because I never want to see it again."

"But, Joslyn—"

"I don't. It's all—it's all over. I don't want to see it; I

don't want to think about it. I don't even want to talk about it anymore."

My mother said gently, "Joe probably didn't mean to hurt you."

"He didn't—"

"Maybe he just wasn't able to respond the way you wanted, the way you expected. People living that deeply inside themselves sometimes forget how to react to other people's feelings."

I thought about that. Then I said glumly, "I don't know. He didn't— I think he saw the one thing in it we all forgot. I saw it in the beginning, but I forgot: that it's just a little, musty room in an empty house nobody wants. And that's —that's what he saw. All the other things were just there trying to hide that. But he saw underneath it all, to the bare boards. That's what he was looking for when he pulled the curtains apart, and that's what he found." My voice hurt as if I had over-used it. "So it just—it just didn't do him any good."

My dad said, "You can't know that. You all did something for him: that's what he'll remember."

"I don't know. He just— I don't know. I don't want to think about it."

In the silence, I heard the clock tick. I heard footsteps on the walk, and I was afraid it was Brian, but they passed. My mother drew a breath. "Well, you may feel a little better about it in the morning. I think we should all go to bed. Did Claudia go home?"

I nodded. "I walked her home. Why?" Then I realized why. "Did Mrs. Gill call?"

"And Mrs. Takaota." She stood up, shaking her head. "At least we knew if you were in trouble, you were all in it together."

I went to bed, but I couldn't sleep for a long time. I opened the curtains and the window, and lay looking out at the roofs and trees, and the handful of stars, scattered at random like freckles across the top of the window. I heard Brian come home softly about an hour later; then, even later, I heard fire sirens in the distance, and I wondered if the deserted house were burning up. I wished it were, so it would just vanish, and we could forget it had ever existed in the first place. Finally, about the time the moon fell out of sight down somebody's chimney, I fell asleep.

I couldn't find Brian the next day when I got home from school. He wasn't in the house or the garage, so I went out front and looked under George Harmon's car. I found his head.

I sat down on the sidewalk and said wearily, "You don't have to blame us. We didn't want to hurt him."

He surprised me by answering. "You didn't." His hand came out, felt around. "Hand me that wrench."

"Then what did we do?"

"Nothing. He found what he expected. Now shut up about it. Here." He dropped a greasy bolt in my hand. There was a soft splat I couldn't place; he rolled out from under the car.

"I'm going to be a mechanic. Going to get me a job in a gas station and learn all there is to know about engines."

"Tomorrow I have to know all there is to know about the past tense in Spanish."

He sighed, but he couldn't find a way out of it. "All right. Let me get this oil changed first."

"I thought you and Joe were going back to school together."

For a moment he wasn't going to answer me, remembering the appalling, silent walk the night before; I saw the sudden anger in his eyes. Then it faded and something else came into his face. He rubbed his nose with a greasy palm. "Joe's not going back to school for a long time."

"What do you mean?" I said. "What do you mean?"

He inched back under the car. "Ask Barbara."

"No!" I knelt down and looked at him under the car. "What do you mean?"

He looked back at me behind a thin stream of oil. Then he came out again and squatted down in front of me. He said quietly, "Joe disappeared this morning. Mrs. Takaota had been staying home with him, and she called to see if he was here. So I said I'd check a few places. I found him down at school, outside the fence around the tennis courts and the pool. His hands were all cut up. One of the teachers had just found him. He— I guess he'd just been holding onto the steel fence so tight he cut himself, and he never even realized it . . ." His voice trailed away. I felt as though something big inside my head were trying to get out, pushing hard at my eyes, my throat.

"Brian! Did we do it?"

He looked as if he were about to cry, too. "I asked Mrs. Takaota. She said no. She said, of course not. She drove us home. Oh, hell." He took the bolt and rolled back under the car. "I don't know. Maybe it's because his father died when he was thirteen. Maybe it's because he's Japanese and stupid kids called him names in grammar school. Maybe he was born with a kinky brain. I don't know. I just don't know." There was a clank, as if the wrench had slipped off the bolt and banged hard against something. "Now quit talking about it. I don't want to think about it anymore. Read your history assignment."

"I don't have one."

"Well, read something! Anything!"

So I conjugated Spanish verbs at him until he finished. Then he came upstairs to help me study. I couldn't concentrate very well, and he lacked his usual money-hungry zeal, but at least he was still speaking to me.

I called Barbara when I finished, to see if she wanted to talk. Her voice was tired, subdued.

"Did you get home okay last night?" she asked.

"Yes. My parents were waiting up for me."

"So was my mother. I didn't want— I had to tell her. Joslyn, Joe had gone to bed, so I didn't have to face him. I didn't—it was a little hard to. And today he—last night Neil came over, after we all went to bed. He said he'd been with Brian before."

"Where did they go?"

"He said they just went to that all-night doughnut shop

where Neil works, and just sat. Like we did, I guess, only they talked. About cars."

"Cars?"

"That's what Neil said. Then Neil came to my house and knocked on my bedroom window, and I went outside, and we talked until almost dawn."

"About cars?"

Her voice loosened a little. "No, just things. Everything except— And then today, Joe—he—Joslyn—"

"I know."

She drew a breath. "Did Brian tell you?"

"Yeah. How is— Is he okay, now?"

"He's watching TV with the twins. Sometimes I think they're the only people he wants to have around. Joslyn, my mother looks so tired." She sounded close to tears. "She doesn't know what to do anymore; she doesn't know how to help him. He's got to go back to that place after a while, and it costs so much, but he's got to go . . . It seems so hopeless . . ."

I agreed, but I said comfortingly, "Maybe he just needs a little more time. After all, they did send him home now."

"Yes, but— Well. Maybe. Joslyn, I still can't—I still can't figure out what we did wrong. I don't understand how we could have been so completely and totally wrong about that room."

"I don't know. But I guess we were."

She was silent a moment; we both were. Then she said, "Well. I've got to help with dinner. I'm glad you called."

"Okay. I'll see you tomorrow."

And that was the last any of us talked about Joe's room for a while. We just avoided mentioning it. Claudia went to have her operation, but I couldn't see her because of the hospital's visiting rules. So I had to be content with phoning her every day. I pinned the hem to Barbara's Junior Prom dress the day she had to wear it, and helped her stitch it up at the last minute; she had been so preoccupied she'd forgotten about it. I studied with Brian every afternoon; my grades were getting better because I didn't have much else to think about. But Brian was never satisfied; he wanted his guitar, and I wasn't making enough A's. He went back to his normal, browbeating techniques, and we had funny squabbles that seemed to draw us closer together; but he never spoke of Joe.

And then, the day after Claudia had come back to school again, we had lunch together, the four of us: Neil, Claudia, Barbara and I, under one of the big pines on the front lawn of the campus. The sky was hot blue; looking up at it, my eyes slid straight across it because there wasn't a cloud to stop them.

Barbara, lying with her head on Neil's stomach, said softly, "Joe's going back tomorrow."

None of us said anything. I had a sudden urge to throw something at something, but all I had in my hand were potato chips, which I was eating. Neil, who had been intently poking grass blades into Barbara's hair, let his hand fall.

He said after a moment, "I took the fish and the sea horse out so they wouldn't die."

I had forgotten about them. Thinking about them made the room fall into place again in my head, piece by piece, the banners, the painting, the candles, the plants. Claudia, on her stomach with her face in the grass, lifted her head suddenly.

"The plants must be dead."

Neil gave a long, slow sigh, making Barbara's head sink. He said wearily, "I couldn't—" Barbara glanced up at him.

"I'm glad you got the sea horse, anyway. By the time I remembered it, I was sure it must be dead. So I didn't—I didn't check. I should have. But I—"

"It's okay." He was still again; his fingers found a stem of crabgrass, snapped it, and tucked it behind her ear. Then he said, "We should take our things out. They might get stolen, and some of them don't even belong to us."

Barbara made a sound and rolled away from him. Her hair swung in front of her face; he reached toward it, but she brushed it back herself and her face appeared, puckered. She nodded, sighing.

"Just one more time," Neil said. I heard footsteps by my ear then, and turned my head. Brian dropped down unexpectedly among us. Claudia's face came out of the grass. I stared at him.

"What are you doing here?"

He didn't answer me; he was looking at Claudia. She

turned red under his gaze. Her nose seemed longer, straighter, and when she smiled, as she was doing then in spite of herself, you hardly noticed the faint blurring of the shape of her upper lip. She had gotten her hair cut, too; it lay short and very smooth against her head. Her face looked older somehow, and thinner. Brian whistled, and she dropped back into the grass.

He said, "Don't do that; I want to see—" But she wouldn't come up.

Neil, turning on his side to face Brian, said, "How'd it go?"

"Oh . . . maybe."

Whatever that meant, it made Neil smile.

I said, "What have you been doing?" He was wearing shoes and a shirt on a hot spring day. He didn't want to answer me, but for some reason he decided to.

"Talking to Mr. Xanthos."

Claudia's head came up. "You going back to school?"

"I don't know. Maybe." Then he looked at her. "He says I can; it's just a matter of making up classes. I'll be a year behind, and I won't like it. I'm not sure I want to go back, but I might. I might try."

"You can do it," Neil said. Brian ruffled his hair.

"The question is: why should I?" His eyes gave Barbara a little, fleeting glance. "How's—how's Joe?"

She shook her head. The bell rang then, and we started gathering our things. She said softly, "Not so good. He's going back tomorrow."

He gave a little nod. "I'd like—I'll come and see him tonight before he goes. Is that all right?"

She smiled. "Sure." She still had all the grass blades in her hair; Neil started brushing them out. I picked up my books with a sigh. Four more weeks and unless I flunked my finals, I wouldn't be a freshman any more. But I wasn't sixteen; I wasn't allowed to ask why, before I was plunged into another year of more of the same only harder. There seemed no end to it.

Then Neil, looking over Barbara's shoulder, said to Brian, "You have a mind. It's for thinking. If you can't use it, you're dead. You've got to start learning how somewhere."

Brian reached down to pick up the empty potato chip bag I had left. He wadded it into a ball absently, looked down at it.

"Maybe."

I couldn't concentrate that night while we were studying. Brian was tossing Spanish vocabulary at me, since I had a test in it the next day, but I got genders wrong and confused words and mispronounced them until Brian, lying backwards on Erica's bed with his feet on the headboard, said with a groan, "We just did this chapter two nights ago! Will you think!"

"I'm trying! Hurry up; I have to—" I stopped. He looked at me.

"What?" But he guessed what. He sat up abruptly. "Now what the hell are you going to try to do?"

I felt my face burn. I said tersely, "We're going to take our things out of the house. And if you say one more word —one more—I'll flunk every test from now till my finals."

"Oh." He subsided, lying back. He propped the book open on his chest. "Umbrella."

But I didn't answer. My face still felt red. He glanced at me and said again, "Umbrella."

"So give me one good reason."

"Huh?"

"Why should I tell you what umbrella is in Spanish? Why should I pass my tests? It's okay if I'm grounded now, I'm not doing much of anything and there's only a few more weeks of school. I don't even like school, so why should I go on? You wouldn't care what kind of grades I made if you didn't want a guitar. That's all you care about. I don't have to study. Why should I? You don't. I've never had such a rotten year in my life. Why should I finish one just to start another one? I'd rather make doughnuts."

He gazed at me, his mouth open, the book fallen forward on his chest. He had to worry; he was going to be out of a job if I went on strike.

Then he said softly, "That's not true. I'll teach you for free from now on."

"Why?" I said suspiciously.

"Because I care. I don't want you to drop out. I wish I hadn't." He picked up the book. "Umbrella."

"*El paraguas,*" I said a little dazed. "Then why don't you go back?"

"Suitcase. Because it's easy to drop out, but hard to go back."

"*El maleta.*"

"*La maleta.* Garden."

"*La jardín.* I'll make A's on all my finals if you go back. And you won't have to teach me for free."

"*El jardín.*" His eyes slid to my face. "You couldn't. Not in algebra."

"Then you're safe saying yes, aren't you?"

He wiggled a little, like a caught fish. "Milk."

"*La leche.* Think of all the money you'd get if I did get all A's. Don't you want me to try? I could just try for C's."

"C's? After all this work?" he said indignantly.

I said, "You want me to work; you have to pay for it. Deal?"

He eyed me. The algebra probably made him feel safe. He licked his lips. Then he gave a little nod. "Deal."

" I want it in writing. And witnessed."

"All right!" He was already nervous, and I grinned. "Now let's get this finished; I want to go see Joe." But he didn't go on; instead he turned his head to look at me again. "I'm sorry I yelled at you like that. At least you tried. I hardly did that much." He went back to the book. "Mailbox."

Neil and Barbara picked me up when it finally got dark. There was no reason for secrecy; my parents knew we had to clear our things out eventually. They might have guessed where we were going, but I didn't tell them; it was still hard to talk about. We stopped for Claudia at her house, then drove to the deserted house in silence. We got there before the streetlamps went on, so we didn't have a problem sneaking in. We stood in the dark living room while Neil groped for his lantern. The house smelled lonely, musty; it felt smaller than I remembered.

Neil murmured, "Can't even remember where—oh." He found it, and we followed him. I had a sudden hope that maybe someone had come and stolen our things, maybe even painted the walls over, hiding our work, so there would be no sign we had ever been in that house. But I knew what we would find when Neil switched on the light: dead yellow plants in hard-packed earth; dust on the candles, the books and shelves; dust balls flitting across the floor as we passed. I wondered if we could get everything out without getting caught. I wondered if Neil had brought a hammer to get the crates off the walls. He switched on the lantern, and I blinked in the sudden light. I wondered for a second why everything looked so strange.

Then I realized that everything was strange because nothing had changed.

"Who watered the plants?" Claudia said.

Barbara looked at Neil. He set the lantern down on the floor, carefully. His face was expressionless. He shook his head slightly. "I didn't. No." He looked at me, but I shook my head. I didn't trust my voice.

"Brian?" Neil suggested. I thought. Then I shook my head again.

"No. No—he wouldn't have."

Barbara had begun to move again. She touched things: the rocking chair, a shelf, the tree. She whispered, "It's all been dusted. And the earth under the tree is still damp. And there are— There are used matches. And—there's a book—there's a bookmark in this book—"

"Even the little plants are damp," Claudia said wonderingly. "And they don't look like— Some of them have really grown. Someone must have come nearly every— Someone—" She stopped. She put her hand to her mouth. "Barbara—"

Barbara stared back at her, her eyes growing wider and wider. She moved suddenly. She grabbed the tree by its big ceramic pot and started shoving it toward the door.

Neil said, "Wait, I'll get it." But she didn't hear.

She said, "He can take it back with him tomorrow. He can put it in his room and water it there, and watch it grow. He-he must have brought water with him all that way, because we didn't have much here. Neil, I can't lift this damn pot."

"I'll get it." He was laughing, as he bent to help her. She wiped her face quickly with one hand, leaving a streak of dirt on it, but it didn't do much good because she was still crying even though she was smiling. Neil hoisted the pot in his arms.

"I thought that lantern had been moved." He turned a little awkwardly as she ran ahead of him to open the door. "Watch it— Someone may be out there—"

"Good!"

The front door banged open. I looked at Claudia, who was still standing with her hand over her mouth. She whispered behind it, "I don't believe it. Do you believe it?"

"No." Then things whirled a little in my head, as if they were colored leaves caught in a gentle wind: things that had happened to all of us, things that hadn't happened yet, but might. Looking at them, I started to smile.

"Well. Maybe."